Awesome Volunteers

Christine Yount

D1169742

Group
Loveland, Colorado

DEDICATION

To Mike, my loving and supportive husband. This book would've been impossible without you.

To my patient children Grant, Abby, and Reed...Now we can play, big time!

And to Max Barnett for your example of following the Leader. It's you times thousands.

Awesome Volunteers

Credits
Editor: Jennifer Root Wilger
Creative Development Editor: Dave Thornton
Chief Creative Officer: Joani Schultz
Art Director: Randy Kady
Cover Art Director: Jeff A. Storm
Computer Graphic Artist: Nighthawk Design
Cover Designer: Randall Miller Design
Illustrator: Matt Wood
Production Manager: Peggy Naylor

Library of Congress Cataloging-in-Publication Data
Yount, Christine.
    Awesome volunteers / by Christine Yount.
       p.   cm.
    ISBN 0-7644-2056-9
    1. Christian education of children. 2. Voluntarism--Religious
aspects--Christianity. I. Title.
BV1457.2.Y67 1998
268' .3--dc21   98-18022
                                                                      CIP

10 9 8 7 6 5 4 3 2   07 06 05 04 03 02 01 00 99

ACKNOWLEDGMENTS

While my family made many sacrifices for this book, we talked about all the benefits it could produce—even if it were read by just one person. We imagined that one person getting such a handle on volunteer recruitment and management that his or her children's ministry would be turned around, children's lives would be transformed, and eternity would be radically altered. I'm thankful to my family for sharing the vision and believing that one reader's ministry was reason enough to give up much when free time was at a minimum—and for loving me through a sometimes grueling process.

And to my extended family who were there when we needed extra help, thanks so much. Thank you Don and Vi Yount and Mickie and Emily McKibbin for your support.

Over and over, I saw God's faithfulness in providing exactly what I needed when I needed it. I'm so grateful for the blessing of my faithful family and friends who volunteered to be my prayer support team throughout this book's birth. Thank you Larry, Terryl, Larryn, and Haley Rayburn; Doug and Patsy Lange; Jerry and Susan McCaskill; and Byron and Heather Ward.

And most of all, this book would never have happened without the many children's ministers who allowed me to peek into and showcase their ministries. I am deeply indebted to these incredible servants of God:

Sandra Anderson
Christ Episcopal Church in
Greenville, Delaware

Betty Baggley
Gospel Tabernacle Assembly
of God in Chickamauga,
Georgia

Judy Basye
First Baptist Church of San
Mateo, California

Judy Cooper
Village Presbyterian Church
in Shawnee Mission, Kansas

Todd Crouch
Worldwide Church of God in
Scenery Hill, Pennsylvania

Paul Duris
East Hill Foursquare Church
in Gresham, Oregon

Mary Eagle
St. Cecilia Church in
Beaverton, Oregon

Mandy Files
Grace Community Church in
Bartlesville, Oklahoma

Darrell Fraley
Hope Church in Cincinnati,
Ohio

Cheryl Hall
East Tulsa Christian Church
in Tulsa, Oklahoma

Dana Janney
Whittier Hills Baptist Church
in La Habra, California

Keith Johnson
Wooddale Church in Eden
Prairie, Minnesota

Selma Johnson
Northway Baptist Church in
Dallas, Texas

Robbie Joshua
Faith Community Church in
West Covina, California

Carmen Kamrath
Community Church of Joy
in Glendale, Arizona

Dann Lies
Living Word Christian Center
in Brooklyn Park, Minnesota

Dwight Mix
Fellowship Bible Church in
Lowell, Arkansas

Debbie Neufeld
Grant Memorial Baptist
Church in Winnipeg,
Manitoba

Bonnie Newell
Breiel Boulevard Church of
God in Middletown, Ohio

Clara Olson
New Hope Community
Church in Portland, Oregon

Heather Olson-Bunnell
St. Mark's United Methodist
Church in Roanoke, Indiana

Cynthia Petty
Lake Pointe Baptist Church
in Rockwall, Texas

Darlene Pinson
Olive Baptist Church in Pensacola, Florida

Kevin Reimer
Lake Avenue Church in
Pasadena, California

Tammy Ross
First Baptist Church in
Columbia, Tennessee

Sondra Saunders
Prestonwood Baptist Church
in Dallas, Texas

Debbie Weisen
Spokane Valley Nazarene
Church in Spokane, Washington

Judy Williamson
St. John's United Methodist
Church in Albuquerque,
New Mexico

Steven Wood
Westwood Church in Evansville, Indiana.

CONTENTS

INTRODUCTION

June

It's summertime and once again time to recruit Sunday school teachers for the coming school year. The big change in our church is that we're going to two services this year-with full children's programs for each service. It's an exciting development because the change has been driven by our burgeoning children's ministry. We've simply outgrown our Christian education facilities.

But the thought of having to recruit twice as many volunteers as before is daunting to our Christian education committee. Will there be enough volunteers who'll step forward for not only one service, but now two services?

July

Thanks to strong support from our church staff and elders, some of our committee's fears have been relieved. This month our church leaders preached a series of sermons about commitment and highly promoted the need for people to give their lives in ministry to children.

August

It's August now, and at last count, we only need two more teachers. That's incredible! Now all we have to do is motivate, encourage, support, train, equip, affirm, and pray for these wonderful volunteers. As hard as recruiting volunteers can be at times, we know the real job is ahead of us. **Lord, help us keep these volunteers.**

S ound familiar? Every time Children's Ministry Magazine asks its readers, "What are your top three concerns?" inevitably people answer something like this: volunteers, volunteers, volunteers. Without a committed cadre of volunteers, effective children's ministry simply couldn't take place. Yet recruiting and keeping volunteers is a struggle for most children's ministers. The openings are rarely completely filled, the volunteers don't always fulfill their commitments, and getting volunteers to come to training meetings is about as easy as getting a child to clean his room (especially if he's eight!).

That's what *Awesome Volunteers* is all about—the fine art of calling people to a significant, lasting ministry with children and managing them successfully. As you apply the principles from this book, you'll turn a corner in your volunteer management that you never dreamed possible. We'll take an in-depth look at how Jesus recruited his disciples and learn how we, too, can implement principles from the Master's plan of volunteer management.

Awesome Volunteers will equip you with the insider secrets to create a dynamic children's ministry program that has people waiting in line to volunteer. You'll learn from the pros how to build a team, pass on a vision, and train volunteers in today's world. And you'll get fun and creative ways to affirm and celebrate volunteers.

I hope that *Awesome Volunteers* will become your best friend and trusted guidebook as you build a winning team to reach children for Christ. Blessings to you in this very important ministry.

Chapter 1

THE MASTER'S PLAN

It was just before the Passover Feast. Jesus knew that the time had come for him to leave this world and go to the Father. Having loved his own who were in the world, he now showed them the full extent of his love.

The evening meal was being served, and the devil had already prompted Judas Iscariot, son of Simon, to betray Jesus. Jesus knew that the Father had put all things under his power, and that he had come from God and was returning to God; so he got up from the meal, took off his outer clothing, and wrapped a towel around his waist. After that, he poured water into a basin and began to wash his disciples' feet, drying them with the towel that was wrapped around him.

He came to Simon Peter, who said to him, "Lord, are you going to wash my feet?"

Jesus replied, "You do not realize now what I am doing, but later you will understand."

"No," said Peter, "you shall never wash my feet."

Jesus answered, "Unless I wash you, you have no part with me."

"Then, Lord," Simon Peter replied, "not just my feet but my hands and my head as well!"

Jesus answered, "A person who has had a bath needs only to wash his feet; his whole body is clean. And you are clean, though not every one of you." For he knew who was going to betray him, and that was why he said not every one was clean.

When he had finished washing their feet, he put on his clothes and returned to his place. "Do you understand what I have done for you?" he asked them. "You call me 'Teacher' and 'Lord,' and rightly so, for that is what I am. Now that I, your Lord and Teacher, have washed your feet, you also should wash one another's feet. I have set you an example that you should do as I have done for you. I tell you the truth, no servant is greater than his master, nor is a messenger greater than the one who sent him. Now that you know these things, you will be blessed if you do them.

—John 13:1-17

"I've set you an example that you should do as I have done for you," Jesus said. Not only has Jesus called us to the awesome task of serving him through children's ministry, but he has also given us his example to follow as we serve.

"I've set you an example that you should do as I have done for you."

It's so simple.

And yet so profound.

As a new Christian in college, I remember hearing for the first time that God had given spiritual gifts to his children—that each of us was specially suited and equipped to carry out the ministries that God would call us to. I was like a child at Christmas! God had given me gifts! It made sense that a loving and giving God would not leave me alone, but rather would bestow upon me special gifts that he made uniquely for me.

I feel a similar sense of elation when I think about how God has provided all that children's ministers need to staff their ministries. And yet so many children's ministers struggle with the task of recruiting and keeping volunteers. As resource-hungry, ever-learning people, we go from one seminar, article, or book to another, searching for the right formula or the no-fail gimmick that'll help us vanquish the volunteer staffing dragon. But alas, all we end up with is fragmented approaches—however creative—that yield immediate results but no real lasting value. What are we doing wrong?

Remember Jesus' words: "I've set you an example that you should do as I have done for you." In this book, I promise you no easy answers—no quick gimmicks. At the very heart of Jesus' model of volunteer management is the cost that he laid out for anyone who chooses to follow him. Mark 8:34 says, "Then he called the crowd to him along with his disciples and said: 'If anyone would come after me, he must deny himself and take up his cross and follow me.'"

> ⌐Quote¬
>
> "When he asks for and receives our all, he gives in return that which is above price—his own presence. The price is not great when compared with what he gives in return; it is our blindness and our unwillingness to yield that make it seem great."
>
> —Rosalind Goforth

Following Jesus isn't easy. It means putting his and others' interests above our own. It means putting to death selfish, misguided, and quick-fix interests. Are you ready to pick up your cross?

A CLOSER LOOK

Let's take a closer look at John 13:1-17 to see what we can learn from Jesus' example.

● **Jesus loved his followers.** John 13:1 says, "Having loved his own who were in the world, he now showed them the full extent of his love." Over the course of his three-year ministry, Jesus repeatedly answered his followers' questions, comforted their fears, provided for their physical needs, and prayed for them. That's love. With Jesus' example in mind, can we really say that we Love our volunteers—with a capital L?

Leith Anderson, senior pastor of Wooddale Community Church in Eden Prairie, Minnesota, says the number-one rule of recruiting, motivating, and stewarding volunteers is to begin with the person.

"Most of us begin with ourselves. We're focused on our busy schedules, limited resources, and personal priorities," Anderson says. "While it's good to be highly focused, it's bad to ignore someone's personhood and want to just use him or her for your purposes."

Anderson suggests that when we recruit volunteers, we should repeatedly ask ourselves, "Who is this person? What does he most need? How can I help her meet her needs through volunteering?" (from the speech, *Stewarding and Motivating Volunteers*).

Jesus said in John 15:13, "Greater love has no one than this, that he lay down his life for his friends." Are we that committed to our volunteers? Or are we just hoping that they'll be that committed to us? Jesus loved his volunteer followers to the fullest extent.

Stop & Consider

Read the gospel of John in your personal devotions. As you read each chapter, list the principles of volunteer management you learn from Jesus' life.

• **Jesus understood his position and role.** John 13:3 says that "Jesus knew that the Father had put all things under his power, and that he had come from God and was returning to God." This Scripture points out a critical principle from Jesus' example and one that may illustrate the importance of dying to self in children's ministry: Jesus understood his role. In other passages of Scripture, we see that Jesus spent the bulk of his time not with the hungering and needy crowds, but with his followers. Jesus spent three years molding, shaping, instructing, loving, and even rebuking his ever-present followers.

And because Jesus was secure in who he was, he was able to humble himself and minister to his untrained, sometimes-doubting volunteer followers by stripping off his outer clothing, wrapping a towel around his waist, and washing grimy feet. Even though he was the Son of God, Jesus served.

Jesus approached ministry differently than most of us do. Instead of always focusing on the many, Jesus primarily focused on just a few people. Even though the crowds desperately needed to hear his life-giving message, he repeatedly left them behind to retreat with his disciples. Jesus understood that as he gave his life deeply to these few, they would be sold on his vision, equipped in his ways, and committed to giving their lives to reaching the multitudes that some could've accused Jesus of neglecting at times. Jesus understood that his greatest ministry would be in a few who would reach a few who would reach a few, all the way to the ends of the earth! Whew!

If the crowds that followed Jesus had been crowds of kids and a children's minister had been around, what do you think he or she would have done? The children's minister would've organized a giant sidewalk Sunday school or kids' crusade. Or planned a huge lunch with a creative visual arts presentation of the gospel. And then the children's minister would've scrambled like crazy to recruit people to reach the masses of children for Christ.

Would you have?

Jesus wouldn't have.

As children's ministers who struggle with the "nasty" task of having to pull "unmotivated, uncommitted, unskilled" adults on board to reach those "precious, innocent, needy" children, we need to change our paradigm. If we, like Jesus, want long-term results in ministry, we must instead view our volunteers as "wonderful, optimistic, needy" co-ministers and make them the primary focus of our ministry. And as we apply Jesus' principles in building a committed team of adult volunteers, the kids in our churches will be doubly blessed.

We all love "our kids." But we're able to love them more and minister to them better when we invest in our volunteers. As you commit to your volunteer team in the same way that Jesus committed to his volunteer team—and this is the premise of this entire book—your ministry to children will increase in its effectiveness and impact.

● **Jesus knew his followers.** Jesus knew that Judas was going to betray him. He even knew that impulsive Peter would resist having his feet washed. I'm sure Jesus knew which disciples liked to sleep flat on the ground and which preferred a pillow. He must've known which disciples liked figs and which preferred dates. He knew his followers' secrets, their fears, their dreams, and their potential.

He knew these things because he did an interest inventory at the beginning of every recruiting phase...NOT!

You know why Jesus knew these things (apart from the fact that he is God). Mark 3:14 says that Jesus "appointed twelve—designating them apostles—that they might be *with* him and that he might send them out to preach." Jesus knew his disciples because he spent time with them.

Cheryl Hall, children's pastor at East Tulsa Christian Church in Tulsa, Oklahoma, understands and beautifully applies this principle. In an interview for Children's Ministry Magazine, I asked her about how she connects

"Every believer in Jesus Christ...is expected to achieve his or her full potential for God. And most of them would if they had the opportunity, if someone would get the food within reach, if someone would give them the help they need, if someone would give them the train-ing they should have, and if some-one would care enough to suffer a little, sacrifice a lit-tle, and pray a lot."

—LeRoy Eims

with her volunteer coordinators in a typical week. Cheryl said, "We eat a lot. Sometimes we shop a lot. We're always doing something for the church. Maybe it's a work day. I've been to a lot of sporting events. You know, various things like that. Or, if their child is hav-ing a problem, I'm involved with that at school."

Jesus did a lot of the same things with his followers. They ate together, traveled together, ministered together, prayed together, discussed together, fished together, and more. They were together! Jesus knew his followers, because like Cheryl Hall, he spent time with them. Not just on the Sabbath—and not just at quarterly training meetings. Jesus was with his followers in the day-to-day stuff of life.

When was the last time you took a volunteer out to lunch? Shared a cup of coffee? Went out for a walk? Jesus called his volunteers his friends, and we should do the same.

OK, OK. So we should be spending more time with our volunteers. Jesus did it. But, come on, we're talking about Jesus—Savior of the world, God of everything. Of course, he could do a full-time relational ministry. He could do anything. I know what you're probably thinking at this point: How am I supposed to pull all this off with the volunteers I have? There's no way I could give that amount of time to all of my volunteers!

You're probably right. But *you* don't have to. You can get others to help you—just as Jesus did.

● **Jesus focused on a few.** The beauty of Jesus' example is that even he didn't spend the same amount of time with all of his disciples. For example, Jesus had five hundred followers who were with him as he ascended into heaven after rising from the dead. How often do we hear about all of these people in the biblical account of Jesus' life and ministry?

Then there are the twelve apostles whom we get to know because they're mentioned more often. And even within this core group, there are three disciples who seem to be part of an even more intimate inner circle.

James, John, and Peter were privy to experiences and conversations with Jesus that the other nine weren't. For example, in Mark 9:2-10, we get a glimpse into Jesus' cultivation of his key leaders. After the Transfigura-tion, Scripture says that "Jesus gave them orders not to tell anyone what they had seen until the Son of Man had risen from the dead. They kept the matter to themselves, discussing what 'rising from the dead' meant." Jesus entrusted to these three followers confidences that only they knew.

No matter how many volunteers you manage, you can follow Jesus' example. The Apostle Paul did. Acts 18 tells how Paul spent time with Priscilla and Aquila, who then discipled Apollos in "the way of God" (Acts 18:26). You, too, can focus on a few who'll focus on a few who'll focus on a few. Ad infinitum!

When you incorporate this "ministry of multiplication" into your volunteer management, you'll discover amazing results over the long haul. Consider these calculations, taking into account that it may take you two years to get volunteers fully established in their faith relationships and ministries. Imagine that you recruit and train two workers every two years.

After two years, you'll have two workers. They each train two more.

After four years, you'll have eight workers. They each train two more.

After six years, you'll have twenty-six workers. They each train two more.

After eight years, you'll have eighty workers. They each train two more.

After ten years, you'll have 242 workers. They each train two more.

After sixteen years, you'll have 6,536 workers. They each train two more.

After twenty years, you'll have 58,832 workers. They each train two more.

Let's suppose you'd never invested in a few who'd invest in a few who'd invest in a few. If you'd recruited one person each day, every day, for thirty years, you'd have only one-third of the workers you'd gain by training each worker to train only two more workers. It just doesn't add up to do ministry by any other way than multiplication!

As editor of Children's Ministry Magazine, I've been privileged to meet children's ministers from all over the world with varying backgrounds, experience levels, and gifts. Invariably, when I meet someone who seems to have a handle on volunteer management, he or she—in one form or another—adheres to a volunteer management philosophy that follows Jesus' example. And the benefits are abundant.

"I've got a waiting list of volunteers."

"We have such low turnover in our children's ministry."

"Our volunteer team is like one big family."

These are the kinds of things that bubble out of volunteer coordinators as they talk about their volunteer teams. And it's all because they've gotten it! They've recognized the brilliance of following the example of

Jesus, who in his three years of public ministry spent the bulk of his time with his "volunteer" team. (Hey, those disciples didn't get paid, you know!)

WHERE TO NOW?

I hope you sense the promise of great things to come in the rest of this book as we illuminate Jesus' pattern, meet people who model Jesus' style of volunteer management, and examine practical ways you can transform your volunteer program. The exciting thing about managing volunteers the way Jesus did is that children need the very thing your volunteers need—to be in meaningful relationships with caring people who love God.

The cost is high to follow after Jesus as you move toward a relational style of volunteer management for your children's ministry. But the rewards are great! Your volunteer team will experience the same kind of eagerness, long-term commitment, and satisfaction as other children's ministry teams have who've followed Jesus' pattern.

In John 13:17, Jesus said, "Now that you know these things, you will be blessed if you do them." Bring on the blessings, Lord!

DISCIPLE-MAKING CHILDREN'S MINISTRY

Kevin Reimer, pastor to children and families at Lake Avenue Church in Pasadena, California, explains how Jesus' model of investing in a few has transformed his church's children's ministry.

"I came into this church acutely aware of the struggles for other Christian education practitioners in finding and keeping volunteers. To solve these problems, I was convinced that the children's pastor's primary role must be framed in terms of equipping.

"I reconfigured our ministry teams at Lake Avenue, because I am not able to invest myself as a discipler into more than a dozen people. I told our ministry team that at one level, we were actually doing the business of recruitment when we disciple and invest ourselves in workers. How? By *retaining* our existing volunteers, we greatly reduce the number of new recruits needed each fall, with the added bonus of improving overall ministry quality and ownership among the workers. Our volunteer retention rate after one year of disciplemaking leadership has improved to 70 percent.

"With 350 volunteers, a discipleship-leadership matrix will more easily facilitate training. When we meet, our ministry teams spend the first hour 'reporting.' Each member has a 'charge' of a dozen or so workers he/she has been in touch with for the purposes of finding out what's happening, becoming aware of prayer needs, etc. A BIG part of the reporting time is group prayer. We want the meeting to form around prayer, not just punctuate it.

"Are there obstacles to overcome in implementing this approach to ministry? Sure there are. The hurdles depend on the church. At this church, the program was suffering from pastoral care. At a basic level, people needed to know that they were valuable and had something to contribute with children. Volunteers here have been very receptive. And the church staff? Well, they wanted the most innovative children's programs in the country—they have given complete latitude in the concept's implementation. Our approach is now informing other volunteer-intensive areas of Lake Avenue Church ministries.

"The biggest obstacle our volunteers face now is fear. For those who are not used to being intentional disciplemakers, it is very risky to phone people you don't know, or to invest relationally beyond superficialities. We spent months working through the *Disciplemaker's Handbook* (InterVarsity Press) in training.

"The most exciting reward about this approach to ministry is in seeing gifted workers return with a higher level of energy and ownership in their ministry. We've seen many people like this, and their children are having a ball. We've had kids in tears about moving up a grade because they're not sure Mrs. Such and Such or Mr. So and So are staying in the existing grade. Kids are connecting with their workers.

"Our hope is that discipleship will also happen in the classroom through discipled workers. If we invest in our primary human resources, we can expect to see the same happen in small groups and classrooms. The relationship kids build with the worker is the key, and we are looking here to pass the baton of relational development in Christ through the worker to the children."

FOLLOW ME

From this time many of his disciples turned back and no longer followed him.
"You do not want to leave too, do you?" Jesus asked the Twelve.
Simon Peter answered him, "Lord, to whom shall we go? You have the words of
eternal life. We believe and know that you are the Holy One of God."

—John 6:66-69

Like Jesus' disciples, we "believe and know" that Jesus is God's Son. We even know that his life and ministry are our best examples of servant leadership. But how well are we following him in our ministries with our volunteers?

For years, Max Barnett has demonstrated Jesus' example—to me and to countless others at the University of Oklahoma. I'll never forget the first night I laid eyes on Max. As part of the announcements at a college campus ministry, a tall, lanky, hayseed kind of a fellow stepped up on the stage. He was wearing overalls and a goofy hat. His mussed hair was part of the act, but the gap between his two front teeth was a permanent fixture. In his best drawl, Max announced a coming event that I can't even remember now.

I was shocked to later find out that this "hayseed" was the director of the student ministry that I would become a part of for the next three years. And I soon discovered that first impressions don't count.

Year after year, this unimposing, focused man had worked with his staff to train a force of student volunteers to reach the University of Oklahoma campus. On top of busy academic schedules, we attended training meetings, led dorm Bible studies, planned retreats, and mentored other students—without complaint.

Whenever Max spoke to us as a group, his message was simple. "There are only two things that are eternal—people and the Word of God," he would say. "Invest your life in those things if you want your life to count."

My life has been shaped by this man and his ministry. His visionary leadership clearly demonstrates the impact of following Jesus' pattern. In

Max's ministry, each student volunteer is energized by spending time with other Christians who are eager to know, love, and follow Jesus Christ. Because of Max's integrity and commitment to Christ, thousands of people now pass on his vision to others.

What about you? When you think about managing your volunteer team, what kind of leader will you be for them? Jesus called his disciples not to a ministry, but to a relationship with himself. " 'Come, follow me,' Jesus said, 'and I will make you fishers of men' " (Matthew 4:19). First the relationship, and then the ministry.

When the disciples heard Jesus' call to relationship, they were eager to drop everything and follow Jesus. "At once they left their nets and followed him," Matthew 4:20 says. There were no complaints of, "I'd really like to, Jesus, but I'm scheduled to work in the fish market this Sunday" or "All I know how to do is fish; I don't think I'm qualified to join your ministry." Jesus' disciples gladly followed, knowing that their lives mattered to their servant leader.

Are you ready for your volunteer team to follow you? What will your followers find if they scratch beneath the surface? A hurried, harried program-oriented taskmaster? Or a caring, concerned, people-oriented servant? A healthy, thriving children's ministry begins with you. (Just a little pressure. Sorry, but it's true.)

SERVANT LEADERSHIP

What is servant leadership exactly? And how do you do it? Let's start with a basic definition. If "servant leader" were found in the dictionary, its definition might look something like this:

servant leader (noun) A servant of God with a mission and the people to accomplish it. Should be focused on enabling the people to accomplish the mission.

If you're in a position of spiritual leadership (such as a children's ministry!), here's good news! God has already provided all the people necessary for you to fulfill his task. And as you pray and listen to God, he'll reveal those people to you. But first of all, God wants you well-suited for servant leadership.

Jesus perfectly modeled servant leadership for his followers. Of course, Scripture is full of examples—enough to fill an entire book—of Jesus' servant leadership. We'll take a look at just a few of these. I urge you to look for other examples of Jesus' servant leadership in your personal devotions.

In John 2:1-11, Scripture tells about a time Jesus attended a wedding feast where the hosts ran out of wine before they ran out of guests. Jesus' mother quickly enlisted her Son's service to solve this embarrassing problem. From this story, we find four examples that illustrate what it means to be a servant leader.

● **Servant leaders serve at all times.** Even as an honored guest, Jesus was "on call" to serve the people around him. Jesus didn't come to the wedding expecting to serve. In fact, when Jesus' mother told him about the problem, Scripture tells us that he asked her, "Dear woman, why do you involve me? My time has not yet come" (John 2:4). But he still served.

Often, it's that way in children's ministry. It's difficult to relax on a Sunday morning or at a church social. People look to you for leadership whenever needs arise—no matter the occasion. As you model a servant's heart in every situation—even when the timing stinks—your children's ministry team will learn from your example what it means to serve.

● **Servant leaders know their resources.** When the need arose for more wine at the wedding, Jesus looked around and discovered six stone jars. He told the servants to fill the jars with water and then draw some out to take to the banquet master.

A servant leader never has excuses for why something can't be done. A servant leader is a problem-solver who looks for ways to use old resources or discovers new ways to meet a need. A servant leader is a "can-do" person who's willing to jump in hands first to help out.

● **Servant leaders serve with excellence.** When the banquet master at the wedding feast drank the wine that Jesus had produced, he praised the bridegroom, saying "Everyone brings out the choice wine first and then the cheaper wine after the guests have had too much to drink; but you have saved the best till now" (John 2:10).

There's no such thing as "good enough" with a servant leader. This kind of leader is always striving to do his or her very best. Such a person takes pride in a job well-done and never (OK, rarely) throws together a program at the last minute. A servant leader has an eye for details because of the difference details make for a quality delivery.

● **Servant leaders work behind the scenes.** Jesus could have performed his first miracle in the presence of the bridegroom and his guests. But he didn't. Instead, he called on servants to assist him. Jesus was content to have no one know that he deserved the credit. He got his glory from God.

There is no way this side of heaven that we will ever know all that servant leaders have done. These kinds of people are usually surprised by attention and are a little uncomfortable with recognition. Because they are visionaries, they understand that the behind-the-scenes work is the stuff

Chapter 2

that keeps the front-line work going. A servant leader is easy for team members to follow because he or she demonstrates over and over that commitment goes way beyond words.

GOOD LEADERS, SERVANT LEADERS

In the speech "Stewarding and Motivating Volunteers" delivered to the Greater Washington Society of Association Executives, Leith Anderson itemized these five qualities of a good leader.

- **"Good leaders come in a great variety."** There is no universal one-size-fits-all job description for leaders. God uses all kinds of people.
- **"Good leaders know where they're going and bring others along."** A leader has a sense of destination, and others want to follow.
- **"Good leaders do what needs to be done."** If they can't do it themselves, they find someone who can.
- **"Good leaders build on islands of health and strength."** Rather than spending their energy focusing on fixing what's broken, good leaders strengthen what's going well.
- **"Good leaders bring the best out of others."** They model Jesus' servant leadership much like a conductor of a symphony. They know how to get every member playing beautiful music for the good of the whole.

Jesus' first miracle at Cana was just the beginning of his servant leadership. Over and over he performed miracles, not to bring glory to himself, but to serve others and, through serving, to glorify God. In John 6:1-14, Jesus again modeled servant leadership as he fed the multitudes by the Sea of Galilee. There are six principles of servant leadership in this story.

- **Servant leaders meet practical needs.** Jesus was in tune with people. He realized that the crowds had been following him around for quite some time and probably hadn't eaten. So Jesus reached out to the people at their most basic level of need—hunger—and he met it.

A servant leader looks beyond his or her personal needs—such as the need to staff programs—and is concerned about the personal needs of team members. Such a leader endears people to himself or herself because people know that they're cared for—not just needed.

- **Servant leaders teach by example.** In John 6:5, Jesus asked Philip, "Where shall we buy bread for these people to eat?" Verse 6 says, "He asked this only to test him, for he already had in mind what he was going to do." Jesus could have just ordered Philip to go buy bread. But by involving his disciples in his act of service, Jesus taught them to trust and follow him.

When a servant leader jumps in with volunteers and spends an entire Saturday painting the nursery rooms or stays until the last person goes home after decorating for VBS, something powerful happens in the hearts of teammates. And servant leaders realize how powerfully their example impacts others.

I will never forget a time I saw servant leadership in action. As a home fellowship leader at my church in Fort Worth, Texas, one of my responsibilities was to meet with my ministry coordinator for training, encouragement, and accountability. On one particular day, I was riding in the car with my coordinator, Seth Gatchell, as he drove down busy Hemphill Avenue. The cars before us swerved to avoid hitting something in the road— a rather large tree branch.

Seth swerved and then pulled off to the side of the road. I sat and watched him dart into the street and drag the branch to the side of the road. To this day, I can never swerve to avoid hitting something in the road without remembering Seth's example of servant leadership. And I have to admit that I always have a twinge of guilt when I don't do something to protect other drivers. Seth taught me by his example that because people are valuable, it was no big deal to be inconvenienced on their behalf.

● **Servant leaders trust God to supply their needs.** Perhaps Andrew was skeptical as he brought the little boy's small lunch to Jesus. However, Jesus received it without so much as blinking an eye. Jesus knew and understood the great power that was available to him from God.

A servant leader understands clearly that we are co-laborers with Christ. As a result, there is never any fear when it comes to God's provision for ministry. As we listen to God's leadership in telling us what he wants to do, we have the faith that God will never abandon us in his work.

Henry T. Blackaby and Claude V. King have peeled back the layers of our human understanding to help us understand this principle. They encourage us to see God's work from God's perspective in their book *Experiencing God*. Blackaby and King use as the basis for their book John 5:17, 19b-20: "Jesus said to them, 'My Father is always at his work to this very day, and I, too, am working...I tell you the truth, the Son can do nothing by himself; he can do only what he sees his Father doing, because whatever the Father does the Son also does. For the Father loves the Son and shows him all he does.' "

Blackaby and King explain that true Christian ministry is figuring out where God is at work and jumping on board to join God in that work. It is not starting a work and begging God to come join it. J. Hudson Taylor, a pioneering missionary to China and the founder of the China Inland Mission, said it this way: "God's work done in God's way will never lack God's supplies" (Carol Pleuddemann, ed., *World Shapers*). A servant leader understands this principle.

● **Servant leaders concern themselves with nuances.** Jesus was about to perform one of his most acclaimed miracles—the feeding of more than five thousand men, women, and children. And yet he wasn't flustered by the humongous task ahead. The first thing Jesus said after receiving the little boy's lunch was "have the people sit down" (John 6:10). Jesus was concerned about the people's comfort.

It's easy (and sometimes necessary) to get caught up in the enormity of things that need to be done to run an effective children's ministry. When it's "show time," our hearts race, perspiration glands pump, and we question whether we've thought of everything. Yet when we're caught up in the big picture, we often miss the little people things—the absent volunteer's sick child, or the "thank yous" to the hands tired from sewing costume after costume. A servant leader continually thinks about the well-being of the people being served.

● **Servant leaders serve thankfully, not grudgingly.** John 6:11 tells us that Jesus took the loaves and gave thanks. He didn't grab them, sigh heavily, and begin breaking them impatiently. He graciously paused to give thanks to his Father.

My mother-in-law, Vi Yount, is perhaps the greatest example I've ever seen of someone with a servant's heart. A few summers ago, our family went to Oregon to visit my husband's parents. Vi cooked, cleaned, shopped, and even did our laundry. And I was guilt-ridden. I kept trying to derail her efforts to serve us because I didn't want to be a burden. I was afraid she might secretly resent that I was unable to help as much as I'd like to because of my children's needs.

Vi would ask how she could help me, and I would try not to need help. Finally one day she looked hurt when I refused her help, so I sheepishly told her about my fears. She explained to me what joy it gave her to serve us and how much it meant to her to be helpful.

My mother-in-law continues to bless me as she serves with a thankful heart. When you serve thankfully, as Jesus did, your volunteers and your ministry will be blessed in abundance.

● **Servant leaders finish the job.** Jesus didn't stop with distributing the bread and fish. After everyone had eaten, Jesus said to his disciples, "Gather the pieces that are left over. Let nothing be wasted" (John 6:12b). And in this final detail—twelve baskets brimming with leftover food—God was glorified yet again.

Isn't it so tempting to lose steam toward the end of a project? I know I do sometimes. There's such a passion at the beginning of a project when God reveals the vision. And then that vision begins to dim as the details of the project are worked out.

I go through a series of stages when I feel called to a big task. First, after feeling called, I have a vision for how God could work in the project. I'm excited about the impact there could be on people, and I'm confident that God will provide everything I need to pull it off.

The next stage hits me when things are getting tough, but I still have enough vision to believe in the project. This is the fearful stage. Can I really do this? What have I gotten myself into? Oh, God, help me!

And then I enter the dark stage. Why in the world did I ever agree to do this? I will never be able to do this! I'm angry at myself for agreeing to such a huge challenge. And I'm angry at anyone who crosses my path. I'm tempted to throw it all together just so I can be done with it. Thankfully, this isn't a very long stage.

The final stage is my 20/20 stage. I return to the place where I remember that God called me to this project, and he will help me complete it. I can point to God's faithfulness along the way as he provided exactly what I needed when I needed it. My faith is bolstered and my commitment to the project returns. Celebration Day—or the due date—finally arrives, and I'm happy that I've given my all to the completion of the task.

I can almost guarantee that you'll travel through similar stages during big projects—perhaps several times before your work is done. Even Jesus went through dark times: being tempted in the wilderness, the betrayal of a friend, and the overwhelming darkness of the cross that caused him to cry out "My God, my God, why have you forsaken me?" (Matthew 27:46b; Mark 15:34b).

But instead of Jesus' cry of "My God, my God, why have you forsaken me?" Luke records these words: "Father, into your hands I commit my spirit" (Luke 23:46). With that, he went on to complete his saving work on the cross.

Like Jesus, a servant leader is always able to return to the 20/20 stage and to continue to co-labor with God to completion. May we keep his example before us as we pass through the bright and dark times in our ministries.

Stop & Consider

Read 1 Peter 4:10. What does it mean to be a servant?
Read Mark 10:42-45 and Galatians 5:13-14. Why should we serve?
Read Philippians 2:3-4; Romans 15:7; and Ephesians 6:7. What are essential attitudes of serving?

Which of Jesus' servant leadership qualities are in your life? Which ones could you ask God to strengthen in your life?

INSPIRED

Harold Bullock, senior pastor at Hope Baptist Church in Fort Worth, Texas, suggests these eight keys for inspired servant leadership.

Idealism appealed to in the volunteer. Find out what the volunteer's dreams and goals are related to ministry. Then work with the volunteer to set large, but realistic goals.

Needs met. When a volunteer's basic needs are satisfied, he or she is able to achieve greater things.

Supply freedom and authority. A volunteer will be motivated in proportion to how empowered he or she feels to complete a task. Be careful of drawing the perimeters too tightly and frustrating someone or too loosely and overwhelming someone.

Potential of person visualized. Ask God to help you see people as he sees them. Encourage people by helping them see what you believe they'll become in the nurture of the Holy Spirit and their ministry.

Interest in them shown. How's their family life, job, schoolwork, hobbies, health, and finances? Ask lots of "get-to-know-you" questions and follow-up questions when you know a volunteer is having difficulty in an area, such as "How's it going with work since we last talked?"

Recognize achievement. Give frequent praise for jobs well-done. For hundreds of affirmation and recognition ideas, see chapter eight.

Example set in dedication. Lead the way. It's difficult for your volunteers to go beyond where you are. Get in the trenches and share your heart so people can catch your contagious enthusiasm.

Develop their abilities. Volunteers are a special breed of people. They give so much of themselves in every arena of life—at home, work, and church. In essence, you're filling up all they've poured out when you invest in developing and training them. This is also a protection from burnout and "short-termer" mentalities.

Chapter 3

CATCHING THE VISION

Jesus answered, "I am the way and the truth and the life. No one comes to the Father except through me. If you really knew me, you would know my Father as well. From now on, you do know him and have seen him."

Philip said, "Lord, show us the Father and that will be enough for us."

Jesus answered, "Don't you know me, Philip, even after I have been among you such a long time? Anyone who has seen me has seen the Father.

—John 14:6-9a

Jesus clearly knew God's direction for his ministry—he was to point people to the Father. "I am the way and the truth and the life," Scripture says. "No one comes to the Father except through me." Direction doesn't get much clearer than that. Yet time after time, Jesus' volunteer disciples questioned their servant leader. Did Jesus ever wonder when his followers were going to "get it"?

> ┌ **Quote** ┐
>
> *"The leader must know, must know that he knows, and must be able to make it abundantly clear to those about him that he knows."*
>
> —Clarence B. Randall

Communicating a vision or ministry direction to volunteers can be tricky. Even with the best leadership (like Jesus'), it can take time for volunteers to catch on and get on board with your big picture goals. "Our greatest challenge in working with volunteers is helping them catch a vision and a passion for teaching and working with children," says Dwight Mix, children's pastor at Fellowship Bible Church in Lowell, Arkansas. "To help them see that children's ministry is ever much as important and vital as any other ministry in the church."

Dwight's children's ministry staff of fifteen oversees two hundred and fifty volunteers. Passing on vision "has to start on the individual level," Dwight says. "Ministry and a heart for ministry travels the road of relationships. That means I have to help my staff see the vision and catch this passion by spending time with them. Then they in turn do the same with volunteers."

If relationships are the road for passing on a heart for ministry, vision is the fuel. What is it that God is calling you to in your children's ministry? A dynamic VBS outreach? A commitment to family-oriented programming?

A thriving nursery ministry? To effectively lead volunteers, you must have a vision for what God wants. That vision, dream, or goal is best communicated in a vision statement.

Vision is "an element of ministry that can really add to and direct programs and ministry as a whole," says Carmen Kamrath, children's ministries director at Community Church of Joy in Glendale, Arizona. "First, pray about God's direction for your ministry, where He is leading you and the community you work with. Second, talk to people about your vision statement before making it concrete; it helps to get others' views, and to keep in mind the people you serve."

Once you've sought guidance from the Lord and from those in your ministry, you'll be ready to draft a vision statement for your children's ministry. If drafting a vision statement sounds like a monumental task, it is. The document you'll create will guide every ministry decision you make for months or even years to come. But the monumental task of drafting a vision statement doesn't have to be a difficult one. Read on for visionary direction!

DEVELOPING A VISION STATEMENT

To demonstrate the process of developing a vision statement, I'll critique a mission statement from Cynthia Petty, the director of grade school ministry at Lake Pointe Baptist Church in Rockwall, Texas. Her children's ministry's vision statement is "Partnering with families to reach and teach children in such a way that they have the greatest opportunity to become fully developing followers of Christ."

As you draft your children's ministry vision statement, consider these three areas: mission, method, and measure. Keep a pad of paper handy so you can jot down notes and relevant Scriptures as you think about these issues.

● **Mission.** It's in this part of your mission statement that you convey your passion. What does God want your children's ministry to accomplish? What has God called your church to? Based on biblical imperatives, what do you believe God is calling your volunteer team to achieve with children? Which Scriptures support your view?

As you consider your ministry's mission, think big! Don't limit yourself to a puny reason for ministry—volunteers won't want to invest their lives in something that doesn't matter. But most people are captivated by a compelling, larger-than-life reason for reaching children. Cynthia's church wants to "reach and teach children in such a way that they have the greatest opportunity to become fully developing followers of Christ." That's compelling.

According to Scripture, God's mission is to redeem or buy back the world through his Son, Jesus Christ. 2 Corinthians 5:19 says, "God was reconciling the world to himself in Christ, not counting men's sins against them." Colossians 1:19-20 says, "God was pleased to have all his fullness dwell in him, and through him to reconcile to himself all things, whether things on earth or things in heaven, by making peace through his blood, shed on the cross."

As you consider what God is calling you to in your children's ministry, surround everything you do with the overarching biblical imperatives that you've received from God. Since I believe that reconciliation is the number-one goal God wants us to pursue, I'm excited to see this aspect in Cynthia's mission statement. I can think of nothing more compelling than affecting people's eternal destiny.

● **Method.** This is the big "how" question of your vision statement. How do you plan to do all that you have a vision for in accordance with God's plan? What is God's plan for reaching the world? And what's your plan for reaching your church and community? Your vision statement needs to contain your method. Cynthia's vision statement clearly states how her church plans to reach children—by "partnering with families."

● **Measure.** How will you know if you've realized your vision statement? Cynthia's team of volunteers will know that they're successful every time they see children reading their Bibles, coming to Sunday school, or showing kindness to each other. These are just a few of the ways children demonstrate that they're becoming "fully developing followers of Christ."

Having specific measures in place helps build a sense of accomplishment as your volunteer team reaches and continues to reach the vision statement. If you have a measure in place to know when you've accomplished your vision statement, you'll be able to celebrate with your team all the times that God has enabled you to do what he has called you to do. Think about the end product you're trying to achieve. Whatever it is, that's what you should jot down as your measure.

Now that we've looked at these three sections of a vision statement, stop and write a rough draft of your vision statement. Perhaps when it's all put together, your vision statement will look something like Cynthia's: "Partnering with families to reach and teach children in such a way that they have the greatest opportunity to become fully developing followers of Christ."

GROUP WORK

Don't stop now! Put your rough draft of a vision statement away. Then pull together your children's ministry leaders—a core of committed volunteers, your ministry coordinators, or your Christian education board. Pull as many volunteers as possible into this process. Then, beginning with prayer, lead your children's ministry leaders in the process you just went through. Work toward consensus as you choose the wording for each area.

Once your group completes a vision statement rough draft, ask, "Is this really what we're all about?" Then edit the statement together. Pick apart every word. Ask, "Is this the best word or is there a better word to describe what we're trying to do?" (This is a laborious task, but it's well worth the process!)

After you've edited your statement, you're ready to critique it by asking the "Why?" question. Form pairs. Designate a reader and a writer in each pair. Have the reader read a phrase of the mission statement. Then have the writer ask, "Why?" As the writer takes notes, the reader must respond with an adequate answer. Then have the reader read the next phrase of the vision statement and the writer ask "Why?" again. Continue this process until the entire statement is read. (Readers and writers may want to switch roles at some point in the process.)

Bring pairs back together, and ask:

● What did you learn about our vision statement as you did this process?

● Are there any gaps in our vision statement? Explain.

● What things—if any—do we need to add to our vision statement?

● What things do we need to delete from our vision statement?

Using these questions as a starting point, work with your group to rewrite your vision statement as necessary. Then pare down the vision statement to its bare bones—use as few words in your statement as possible while still retaining the meaning you want.

RATING YOUR VISION

According to Alan E. Nelson in *Leading Your Ministry*, you can rate any vision on these three qualities:

Intensity. What impact will the vision make and how urgent is it? How committed is the leader to the vision? In their book *Built to Last*, James C. Collins and Jerry I. Porras advocate developing a Big Hairy Audacious Goal (BHAG, pronounced Bee-hog). They write, "A true BHAG is clear and compelling and serves as a unifying focal point of effort—often creating immense team spirit. It has a clear finish line, so the organization can know when it has achieved the goal; people like to shoot for finish lines."

Clarity. How clear is the vision in the mind of the leader? A more clear vision will increase the chances of the vision becoming reality.

Size. No one wants to jump on board a puny vision. People want to feel that their lives have counted for something significant. As Collins and Porras write, "A BHAG engages people—it reaches out and grabs them in the gut. It is tangible, energizing, highly focused. People 'get it' right away; it takes little or no explanation." Vision needs to be big enough to capture people's faith and their commitment.

VISION CASTING

Now that you and your leaders know where you're going, you want everyone involved in your ministry to have complete, passionate, to-die-for ownership of your mission. How do you accomplish this?

1. Memorize your vision statement. And not just you. Have your ministry leaders memorize the vision statement also. You want your team to be able to articulate the vision whenever a parent or potential volunteer inquires about your ministry.

2. Set goals according to your vision statement. "Once you have established a vision statement, develop goals that meet that vision and then communicate it to the community you serve," advises Carmen Kamrath. "Once you know your vision, what God has called your ministry to be, it is easier to focus and establish goals for your ministry, for your staff and for you."

⌐Quote¬

"Vision is the art of seeing things invisible."

—Jonathan Swift

3. Broadcast your vision statement. Put it everywhere—on posters, fliers, brochures, business cards, stationery. You can pay a professional designer to do this for you, or you can use a simple desktop publishing software, such as Microsoft Publisher or ClarisDraw to create great promotional pieces.

4. Partner with your pastor. Make sure your senior pastor has a copy of your vision statement. (You'll probably want to do this before you start broadcasting it to others in your church!) If you can make a raving fan out of your pastor, communicating your vision to your volunteers will become much easier. Steven Wood, minister of Christian education at Westwood Church in Evansville, Indiana, has a number-one fan in his pastor. Steven says,

"Over the years I've learned a few things about pastors. First, they hate surprises. As the one who is charged with seeing the 'big picture' for the whole congregation, the senior pastor needs to be informed about what's happening in the children's ministry. I make it a point to give my pastor a copy of anything that goes out in print, whether it's a flier, a handout, a poster, a letter, whatever...he gets a copy.

"I provide him with written scope and sequence plans for all of our children's ministries. That way he knows what's being taught during any given week. If the plan changes for whatever reason, I give him an updated copy. He also gets a written roster of the ministry teams for each children's program.

"The second thing I've learned about pastors is that it's their responsibility to seek the Lord's vision for the church and then communicate that vision to the rest of us. Our task is to get a grasp of that vision and then figure out how we can fit in with it and carry out part of it. My pastor and I meet weekly for prayer and simply to touch base. I know how very busy he is, so I come to that meeting with some things in mind that are worth his time. He works hard to communicate the overall vision and I work hard to communicate how those ministries in my area are going to fit in with that vision."

5. Call people to the vision. When you recruit volunteers, call them to become part of the vision—not just part of your children's ministry. For example, Cynthia Petty could say to a volunteer, "Would you like to teach our second-grade Sunday school class?" That's calling people to a role in ministry. Or she could ask, "Would you like to partner with the parents of our second graders to help these children become fully developing followers of Christ?" Do you see the difference? The second way is calling people to the big picture.

Darlene Pinson, children's director at Olive Baptist Church in Pensacola, Florida, has called her volunteers to the vision. Darlene says, "Our volunteers love the Lord. They understand the great privilege they have to teach the next generation of church leadership."

But passing on vision has been a challenge for Darlene—as it is for most of us. She says, "It's a challenge to help volunteers catch the vision of the importance of training children appropriately." Darlene has capitalized on getting people who've owned the vision to call others to the vision. "To do so," she says, "we have testimonies from children's teachers and we ask potential teachers to observe in a classroom."

6. Train your volunteers in your vision statement. "I have dedicated, faithful, and responsible workers and teachers," says Dann Lies, children's pastor at Living Word Christian Center in Brooklyn Park, Minnesota. "We have an annual meeting with all the workers and go over the vision for the year before and how we did fulfilling the vision. We then set the vision before them for the following year. We have a meeting six months later to check up on how we're doing."

Dann also records the vision for his children's ministry on cassette tapes. Then he gives tapes to new and prospective workers so they'll know what they're signing on for.

7. Use your vision statement as a filter for decisions. Don't just file your vision statement under V. Keep it at the forefront of your mind, and use it to make sound judgments that'll keep your ministry focused on what God has called you to do. For example, if someone in Cynthia's ministry has a great idea for an arts program to help kids understand various media forms, Cynthia's volunteer team could evaluate that in light of their vision statement and determine that it doesn't fit their vision. However, if someone's idea for an arts program has the focus of reaching unchurched children and teaching them how the arts could help them follow Christ, Cynthia would be hard pressed not to seriously consider such a program—in light of her ministry's vision statement.

Your volunteers will appreciate your single-minded, focused leadership when you live out your vision statement.

SLO-O-O-W GOING

What do you do when you feel that you have a vision of where God wants you to go and people are dragging their feet to move toward it? You can see the promised land; you may have even tasted it in previous ministries, but your volunteers want to wander around in the wilderness. What's a children's minister to do!?

First of all, cry out to God. That's what Moses did when he was in the wilderness—more than once. In Exodus 17:4, when the Israelites complained that they had no water, Moses was frustrated to the point of crying out, "What am I to do with these people? They are almost ready to stone me."

But they didn't. (And your volunteers probably won't either.) When Moses cried out to God, the Lord answered and provided for the people's needs. Sometimes we just need to set our plans and schedules aside and wait on the Lord. Psalm 27:14 says, "Wait for the Lord; be strong and take heart and wait for the Lord." And Proverbs 20:22b says, "Wait for the Lord, and he will deliver you."

┌─ **Quote** ─┐

"Beware of harking back to what you were once when God wants you to be something you have never been."

—Oswald Chambers

Kevin Reimer knows what it's like to wait on God's timing. "You have to know the threshold for change in your church situation," says Kevin, pastor to children and families at Lake Avenue Church in Pasadena, California. "Any local church is a system of interdependent individuals. As an ecosystem, it has a threshold for change beyond which there is a significant disruption in the system's ability to maintain its equilibrium. In other words, don't push change until you know where the threshold lies. Once a system loses its equilibrium, stress comes cascading in to a point where people begin acting and thinking erratically. Change that is pushed beyond this threshold will invariably fail."

Kevin understands the need to move slowly in shifting his church's children's ministry from task-orientation to relationship-orientation. "At Lake Avenue, I spent months of observation and prayer in assessing our readiness to change in our leadership structures," Kevin remembers. "Fortunately for us, change was sorely needed in children's ministries, and we had much room to maneuver."

Where is your church's threshhold for change? How much room do you have to maneuver? Are you ready for full steam ahead? Or will you need to engage in more waiting and praying before change can take place? Remember, "Wait for the Lord, and he will deliver you."

When you feel the time is right to move people toward the vision, you're ready to explore change processes that'll help you transform your ministry under God's leadership. In *Leading Your Ministry,* Alan E. Nelson suggests the following five signs that people are ready for change.

Is there a strong sense among the most influential people that change is needed?

Is the group dissatisfied with the present status?

Is there a desire to expand the ministry base to be more effective?

Is there a crisis or significant change in the ministry group?

Do you have a divine insight that significant change is needed right away?

Once you've answered these five questions, Nelson suggests five steps for implementing change.

Know where your people are. Determine the level of support you have for the change. If the change needed has widespread support, you can move rapidly. If the change has sporadic support, meet with specific influencers to have them own the vision. If there is very little support, spend more time in dialogue, gaining interest, and bringing people on board to the vision.

The Christian education board at our church is an incredible group of volunteers; we have no paid staff position for children's ministry. These people are very committed, very busy, and very motivated. My dream is that our board will move to a relational approach to volunteer management. When I suggested that each of us have a team of one-sixth of our volunteers, which would be about seven people each, I got varying responses. Three already-busy people felt there was no way they'd ever have time for that, and the other two were fearful of their abilities to do such a ministry.

Create dissatisfaction. People change primarily for two reasons: dissatisfaction with the way things are and a desire for something different. Create discomfort without appearing negative or condescending. Paint a picture of the future that makes the change irresistible.

At our church, my husband, Mike, and I are trying to put things in place that create a heart cry in our volunteers for more relational ministry. We've been able to have monthly teacher enrichment meetings with our volunteers. In these times, we focus on the importance of being part of the larger team, having relationships with one another, and drawing support from one another.

Provide the solution. Once the problem is acknowledged, people will more readily adopt an answer. Where you're headed should be appealing because it's better than where you are.

Organize and plan the change. If you help people understand the details and what'll be expected of them up front, you'll alleviate their fears. Involve your ministry leaders in developing the details to make the change.

It's been incredible to watch how our volunteers are connecting with one another and appreciating this new approach. Once, one of our volunteers told the people in her age-level group, "I need to hang out with you more!" We celebrated this small change in perspective that'll move us into future changes.

Follow-through is vital. "Plan your work, and then work your plan." If you don't produce at this stage, it'll be very difficult to ask your team to follow you into any proposed changes in the future. But if you follow through and carry out your vision, you'll be well on your way to the promised land.

WHEN HEARTS ARE HARD

Just as Moses encountered the hard-hearted Pharaoh, you may encounter people in your ministry who are simply unwilling to "let go" and let you make the changes necessary to carry out your vision. What do you do when people are simply unwilling to change their ministry paradigm? Darrell Fraley, children's pastor at Hope Church in Cincinnati, Ohio, says, "It's painful because you have to willingly place your vision for the ministry on the chopping block. You also have to understand that your vision for the ministry in that particular church may not be God's vision for that church's ministry. You have to die daily. When the people who are unwilling to change see that you're willing to die to self, they won't be so threatened and over a period of time they'll compromise as trust is built."

Sadly, if you're convinced your vision for children's ministry is from God and if you've tried to lead people toward the promised land but they're still "stuck in Egypt," you may have to admit that it's time to move on. Says Darrell, "There does come a time, though, if the anti-change element begins deflating your enthusiasm and spiritual energy in a harmful way that you need to say, 'Thank you very much. God bless you, but it's time for me to move on to a place where I can be fulfilled in serving in children's ministry.'"

Only God can give you wisdom to know when that time comes.

Stop & Consider

Read Psalm 40:1-3, Isaiah 40:18, and Micah 7:7. List any elements of your vision for ministry you'll wait for God to accomplish. Keep your list handy; then note how God accomplishes his purposes through you and your ministry team.

A VOICE CRYING IN THE DESERT

Carmen Kamrath, children's ministries director at Community Church of Joy in Glendale, Arizona—one of the fastest growing churches in America—explains her visionary leadership.

"Our vision at Community Church of Joy children's ministries is 'to create the most innovative and imaginative children's ministry, bringing the love of Christ to a new generation.' We first developed our vision in a formal way about two years ago. At that time, our children's ministries team brainstormed what we felt God's call was for children's ministries at Joy. We discussed values and goals in the context of our church's vision, which is 'to create the most imaginative twenty-first-century mission center—bringing Joy to the world.'

"Once we developed a vision statement, we mapped out a strategic plan with goals and action steps for five years. These were not cemented in stone; we have refined and added along the way. But our goals gave us direction...in thinking about the future and where we were heading. Each year we review goals as a team; we add, refine, and delete as needed.

"When spreading the 'vision' of children's ministries at Joy, we try to incorporate it into all we do. It is important for our children's staff to 'walk the walk, and talk the talk.' When we are excited and enthused about ministry, it is contagious. That is not always easy for church staff to do! We always remind people of our vision either in our training meetings, fliers and mailers, or just by having it posted where they can see it every time they enter our offices.

"We believe that our ministry reaches beyond the kids; it is also ministry to people who serve and volunteer within children's ministries. So when we are recruiting for volunteers, we let people know how fun it is working with kids! We have volunteers who have 'experienced' the vision and are living it. Once people have experienced the vision, when they have been touched by the ministry personally, they feel ownership. People continue to buy into the vision when they become involved in the relational community of children's ministry. These people will be your best advocates and publicity for spreading the vision of your ministry.

"The most fun part of communicating the vision for me is spreading it to the community. We make a very direct point to reach our community; it is a conscious decision and value. It coincides with the vision and mission of our church, and our volunteers know it's important. We teach our volunteers how to reach out to their community and friends, and why it's important to welcome new kids and make parents feel safe and comfortable.

"Probably the biggest challenge in being a visionary is to always remember the vision. There are times, and they can be often, when ministry is just tough and you want to give up. To remember the vision, to remember what we are all about, is not always easy. There are times when we can feel misunderstood, like those days when you get reamed out by a parent, or volunteers don't show up, or a big roadblock gets thrown in front of you.

"I also think that everyone's gift is not to be a visionary. There are times when I can become so focused on the vision and where we are going that I can forget the details of how to get there. Visionaries need to surround themselves with a team that is supportive of the dream, but also can commit to details or making sure the plan is carried out.

"We have a team like that in our children's staff. I am more the visionary and dreamer while my assistants are more detail-oriented and practical. And that is specifically why I chose them to be part of the team, because we complement each other in the best way.

Chapter 4

GO, TEAM!

After this the Lord appointed seventy-two others and sent them two by two ahead of him to every town and place where he was about to go.

He told them, "The harvest is plentiful, but the workers are few. Ask the Lord of the harvest, therefore, to send out workers into his harvest field.

The seventy-two returned with joy and said, "Lord, even the demons submit to us in your name."

—Luke 10:1-2, 17

The foundation of Jesus' approach to working with volunteers is the team—even if that team is no more than two people. Jesus always sent his disciples out in ministry teams. In fact, one of the only accounts in Scripture that we have of the disciples being alone was when they were scattered after Jesus' arrest (Matthew 26:56; Mark 14:50).

Scripture also tells us what happens when the team splits. Downcast, frightened, and alone, Peter lost sight of the ministry he'd eagerly participated in just hours earlier. When volunteer Peter was asked about his connection to his servant leader, Jesus, Peter repeatedly denied that he even knew him. Contrast that with the seventy-two sent out in pairs who, with each other's support, were able to complete even the most difficult tasks with joy.

Scripture is clear that it's not good to be alone. In Hebrews 10:25, believers are encouraged, "Let us not give up meeting together, as some are in the habit of doing, but let us encourage one another." Ecclesiastes 4:9-12 says, "Two are better than one, because they have a good return for their work: If one falls down, his friend can help him up. But pity the man who falls and has no one to help him up! Also, if two lie down together, they will keep warm. But how can one keep warm alone? Though one may be overpowered, two can defend themselves. A cord of three strands is not quickly broken."

> ┌ **Quote** ┐
>
> *"The biggest disease today is not leprosy or cancer. It's the feeling of being uncared for, unwanted—of being deserted and alone."*
>
> —Mother Teresa

"United we stand, divided we fall," the old saying goes. In today's fast-paced world, perhaps more than ever before, volunteers are looking to form meaningful, lasting relationships. "Relationships have become extremely important in almost every aspect of late twentieth century life," says Leith Anderson, pastor of Wooddale Community Church in Eden Prairie, Minnesota. As evidence of the growing importance of relationships, Anderson points to the changes in modern culture's TV shows. The old shows, such as *Dr. Kildare* and *Marcus Welby, M.D.* were all about individual heroes. In more recent shows such as *ER* and *Chicago Hope,* the hero is the team. And the most highly rated TV shows, Anderson points out, are all about relationships: *Seinfeld, Friends, Mad About You,* and *Frasier.*

Anderson asserts that "many people volunteer not because of the task but because of the opportunity to make friends." That's why team-building is critical to having long-term volunteers. And that's exactly why Andrea Shintaku, a first-grade teacher and one of ten thousand members at Community Church of Joy in Glendale, Arizona, volunteered. She says, "I guess what really motivates me is when you're part of a big church like Community Church of Joy, to make it small you have to participate in things."

Lacking a team network of support, George Kunzle, a volunteer at Whittier Hills Baptist Church in LaHabra, California, quit. "Our church has a two-hour setup where you go to church service in one hour and then you teach in the other hour. So after a few years, you begin to feel isolated from your adult friends, and it's nice to get back in adult relationships."

But the children's ministry staff at Whittier Hills is shifting to a team approach. LuAnn Robinson, a volunteer fifth-grade coordinator at this church says, "Being on a team is really important to me. I don't think we had as much of a team thing before, but they're trying to do more now. For a long time, you kind of felt like the Lone Ranger out there, and it was hard to keep going; kids don't come up to you and say, 'Mrs. Robinson, that was just such a wonderful lesson you taught; it really changed my life.' It's nice to have your peers reminding you that you're doing a good job, you're making a difference. I think it just gets real hard to keep doing it without any team.

"You don't want any of your volunteers to find their jobs 'real hard.' You've worked hard to recruit them; you want to keep them. So if a team approach would make their jobs easier, it's worth implementing—if only for their sanity's sake. But organizing volunteers into teams can also benefit your overall ministry. Here's how."

• **Teams provide balance and cross-training.** No single volunteer has everything he or she needs, no matter how experienced. For example, you may have some volunteer teachers who possess a wealth of Bible knowledge, but lack people skills. Some workers may be great with kids but lacking in organizational skills. With a team approach, volunteers build on each other's strengths. Each team member is strengthened and developed by the other teammates.

● **Teams improve planning and follow-through.** Business executives and other leaders nearly always surround themselves with strong teams. The leader can then present an idea in a meeting with his or her team and let the team attack it, probe it, and offer suggestions. When the meeting is concluded, the whole team is ready to follow through on the revised—and often improved—plan. Teammates can also offer ideas for discussion in this manner.

● **Teams generate energy among volunteers.** Team effort multiplies the individual thrust, provides the impact of sheer numerical strength, and supplies power in attacking a single target. When attacked by a team, a problem that seemed insurmountable to an individual volunteer can be solved quickly, allowing the individual and other team members to move on with their duties. Even huge tasks seem manageable for teams who have got "all hands on deck."

"Teams increase people's ability to accomplish tasks" says Selma Johnson, the minister to children/family life at Northway Baptist Church in Dallas, Texas. "My greatest challenge is keeping the vision going and realizing that volunteers are only going to give so much time to the task and meetings. So we've developed teams throughout the preschool/children's division. This gives teachers ownership in what's going on. We have teams for everything from resources to decorating, recruiting, hospitality, and more."

● **Teams provide opportunities for leadership training.** Team participation provides opportunities for potential leaders to try out their skills at leading, planning, and coordinating. Since leadership is largely a matter of helping others accomplish their objectives more effectively than they could by themselves, people who are expected to be leaders will benefit by the team experience. And as leaders develop, your ministry will continue to grow.

Robbie Joshua, children's minister at Faith Community Church in West Covina, California, has reaped the benefits of using teams in her ministry. She says, "It's important for people (especially in a behind-the-scenes ministry like children's ministries) to know that they're not alone. Team members can encourage one another, support one another, and create with one another. I believe that a productive team is always greater than the sum of its parts."

FROM ME TO WE

How do you go about assembling a productive team? Typically, God lays a vision for a ministry on one person's heart. Then he calls a team of people to fulfill that vision. In Acts 16:9-10, Luke writes, "During the night Paul had a vision of a man of Macedonia standing and begging him, 'Come over to Macedonia and help us.' After Paul had seen the vision, we got ready at once to leave for Macedonia, concluding that God had called us to preach the gospel to them." Only Paul saw the vision, but "we"—Paul's volunteer team—"got ready at once." Paul needed his companions and partners in ministry to help him fulfill the vision.

Just as Paul relied on his ministry partners, we need to rely on our volunteer teams—and encourage them to rely on each other. A team talks about "we" instead of "me." It's "our" instead of "mine." Team members sink or swim together.

A successful team usually consists of no more than eight to ten members, and includes the following elements: an accepted leader, a common goal, a certain division of labor within the group, and a strong sense of commitment and loyalty among team members. "A productive team with a clear vision, working toward a common goal creates momentum," says Robbie Joshua. "Momentum is an important ingredient in achieving success. I believe that momentum creates excitement that will facilitate a vision and help a ministry break through complacent and stagnant barriers that tend to cause burnout."

Let's take a closer look at these elements as you work to beat volunteer burnout and assemble productive teams with your volunteers.

● **Productive teams have an accepted leader.** Debbie Neufeld, children's minister at Grant Memorial Baptist Church in Winnipeg, Manitoba, tells how she develops team leaders from her 150 volunteers.

"I depend very heavily on my team leaders to keep our children's ministry going. They are the ones who work closely with me in finding the right people to serve in their departments; they look after the needs of their staff and the kids and parents that they minister to; they keep me aware of things that I need to know. I try to give the ministry away to them and tell them that the department is theirs to look after.

"I try to meet monthly with my team leaders so we can connect and plan on a regular basis. I have found this to be a hard commitment even for my dedicated workers as they lead such busy lives today and have jobs

> ┌ **Quote** ┐
>
> "The most important measure of how good a game I played was how much better I'd made my teammates play."
>
> —Bill Russell

and families as well...I feel it is very important to keep in touch with my team leaders, even if it has to be on the phone, at least once every week or two."

Mandy Files, director at Grace Community Church in Bartlesville, Oklahoma, agrees: "To help my volunteers realize the importance of their ministry to children I have to spend time with them—even those who are extremely busy. One of my teachers is a full-time mom (kids' ages four, seven, nine, twenty, twenty-two) and a full-time physician. We walk early each morning and spend time talking through her class and potential problems."

It takes time to cultivate leaders among your volunteer teams. And it may not be easy to get into the habit of regular meetings with team leaders. But by spending time with your leaders, you encourage them to develop the same kind of relationship with their team members—volunteers who deserve the same level of time and attention, but may not be able to get it from you. (There are only so many hours in a week!)

Instead of dividing and dividing your time until each volunteer has only a few precious minutes, try multiplying your leadership by spending time with the leaders of your volunteer teams. Ruth Welty, a volunteer at Grant Memorial Baptist Church in Winnipeg, Canada, says, "I've replaced myself a couple of times and that was my prayer. At Grant, those who are in leadership are encouraged to bring somebody alongside to train. That's what I mean by replacing myself—training somebody to do what you're doing so the ministry can grow and develop. If you need to leave, then you're not leaving a big hole."

Second Timothy 2:2 says, "And the things you have heard me say in the presence of many witnesses entrust to reliable men who will also be qualified to teach others." Debbie Neufeld adds, "Just as we pass our faith along to our children from generation to generation, we must also multiply our ministry by sharing it with other reliable people who can then branch out and reach more people."

● **Productive teams share a common goal.** Remember the three Ms: mission, method, and measure? With your children's ministry vision statement in mind (preferably even in view!), each volunteer team should establish its goals. Team goals should include detailed, reachable objectives that advance your children's ministry's vision statement.

Team members must be dependent on each other for achieving their common goal. For example, you may have a volunteer team whose goal is to find the best possible Sunday school curriculum for your church's four- and five-year-olds. Different team members might review curriculum to assess Bible content, age-appropriateness, ease-of-use, quality of artwork, price, and other considerations. While each team member will look for the curriculum that best meets his or her assigned criteria, the team decides together which curriculum best meets the needs of the four- and five-year-olds in your church—the team's common goal.

● **Productive teams employ a certain division of labor.** Exactly who does what on the team? Delineating clear roles provides greater ownership and enables people to excel in their area of responsibility. Before assigning roles, team members should spend some time getting to know each other. Understanding team members' strengths, weaknesses, and personalities will help teams better determine who should fill which role. Keith Johnson, pastor to children at Wooddale Church in Eden Prairie, Minnesota, remembers: "A wonderful way a simple team of two can work together was illustrated by Shea and Gail's interest in working in vacation Bible school. Shea was the party girl, running a wonderful carnival in past vacation Bible schools. Gail had a quiet diligence about her and usually maintained precise schedules and an ordered life. They both decided to co-direct our VBS because they complemented one another. Shea was not organized and Gail was. Gail typically stuck with ideas she knew about, how it had been done before rather than venture out creatively. Gail needed Shea's innate creativity and frenetic energy. Shea needed Gail's calm ordered categories to give structure to original brilliance. Our VBS needed both to make it a balanced outreach that was fun yet organized, having high energy yet stable reflection."

Like Shea and Gail, your teams are peopled with diverse individuals each looking for a place to shine. Dividing labor and assigning individuals tasks within their areas of expertise will keep your teams—and your ministry—shining brightly.

● **Productive teams foster a sense of loyalty and commitment.** One of your volunteers' primary needs is to be needed. Tell them often, "I need you to reach children. I cannot do it without you!" People want to feel that they're making a valuable contribution to the team—that if they weren't a part of the team, there would be a huge gap. "I've noticed over the past three years that we have retained volunteers longer because they feel valued and know that there's a 'place' for their unique gifts and talents," says Robbie Joshua.

In addition to hearing positive feedback from you, it's also important for teammates to communicate to one another how important they are. You can do this in team meetings where team members regularly share "words of appreciation" about what they value in their teammates. Or encourage "holy gossip" where teammates report to the others the great ways they've seen each other contribute.

Team members who feel they're a valuable part of the team are much more likely to remain loyal to your ministry. Here are three more activities that will build community and foster loyalty among your volunteer teams.

● **Play together.** The team that plays together, stays together. When was the last time your team relaxed together? You can build community within your team by planning regular times where your team can kick back and simply enjoy being together. You may decide to play a wild game of Lazer Tag. Or your team may enjoy meeting at a trendy coffee shop on a Saturday morning. Encourage team leaders to find out from their team what they would most enjoy and to plan regular times that are just for fun. As people see how much fun your teams are having in and around children's ministry, they'll want to get on board.

Team playtimes are also great opportunities for leaders to see things they need to be praying about and perhaps working on with team members. While I was in seminary, I attended a wonderful church with an active singles group. For one singles outing, we went to an ice rink to play broom hockey. I tend to be a little competitive at times, so when the other team was getting all the big guys, I cried out, "Hey! That's not fair! We need some big guys too!" A young college student who was the victim of my complaining said, "You know, God has been convicting me lately of whining."

Oops! It's amazing what'll bubble up out of people when you get them out of their comfort zone. Team leaders can prayerfully watch for growth needs in their teammates as they play together.

● **Make prayer a priority.** How much time does your team spend in prayer? Does your team have regularly scheduled prayer times? Prayer will not only bind your team together, it'll help your team members give their heart to the children they pray for.

Prayer is an important part of East Tulsa Christian Church's children's ministry team. "We recently had a day of fasting and prayer," says their director, Cheryl Hall. "We have two or three days throughout the year to keep us focused and to keep us listening to what is true."

Teams can pray together as a group, develop a prayer chain, or have prayer partners within their team. They can pray for the materials they prepare, the children they teach, or the families they reach. They can intercede for the needs of your children's ministry, the needs of team members, and the needs of their families. And they can thank God for all the blessings he's sent your way. The sky's the limit! Prayer helps a team recognize its utter dependence on the power of God, and reaffirms the team's trust in God's miraculous working in and through its ministry.

● **Serve each other in love.** Nurture an environment where team members make sacrifices for one another, serve one another, and meet each other's needs. By God's grace, your goal is to create teams that become the most life-giving source in a teammate's life. Robbie Joshua shares how one of her children's ministry teams served one another.

Robbie says, "This past year one of our team members died suddenly. She was a beautiful Nigerian lady who lit up the room when she walked in. She was in this country finishing her education and planning to return to Nigeria to her husband and children. When her team members became aware of a lack of finances surrounding her death, they immediately collected money to help send the body back to her country to be buried."

I can't help but imagine that God carried the grieving family through this time because of the loving commitment of a children's ministry team that knows what it means to weep with those who weep. That's the kind of team every volunteer longs for.

Volunteers who play, pray, and serve together are likely to feel a sense of loyalty to the team. They won't want to let the team down by failing to show up or failing to complete an assignment. And they're also more likely to stick around.

"We ask for one-year commitments from all our children's ministry workers," says Debbie Neufeld. "We ask them at the end of each year if they will be returning the following year. We have been fortunate to have very committed people as leaders and team leaders over the years who are serving in the children's ministry because they feel called to be there. I encourage my team leaders to stay on for at least two years as the first year is a learning year."

The longer volunteers remain part of your ministry, the more likely it is that they'll develop the skills they need to move to the next level—leading and motivating other team members.

THE NEXT LEVEL

Of course every team needs a leader. But leaders don't exactly grow on trees. It's possible that your ministry may be blessed with natural leaders, but most of the time team leaders require cultivation and training. Keith Johnson shares the ongoing process he goes through with developing leaders:

Quote

"The best leaders are grown, not grabbed."

—Clarence W. Jones

"I take my team leaders to lunch once a month to connect and socialize. It is expected that these undershepherds in turn develop five (at least) volunteers who become their leadership team. They recruit this leadership team and meet with them monthly. I expect them to transfer to those leaders the passion to develop their own leaders, believing the principle that people stick to a ministry when they're hooked to a team."

Keith uses the following topics and questions to generate discussion when he meets with his team leaders. You may want to revise or add questions to adapt this process for the volunteers in your ministry.

SPIRITUAL FORMATION

- How will I help to form Christ in you?
- How are you growing spiritually?
- What's the one question you should be asked that would help keep you growing and on God's path? Who is asking you this question?
- What helps you to live as Jesus would if he were in your place?

VISION DEVELOPMENT

- What next step of the vision do I need to cast for you?
- How are you casting the vision for evangelism with your lead teachers and small group leaders?
- How is your team reaching out to new kids and parents? How can you challenge your team members to do this better?
- Can your leaders articulate the gospel message appropriately? Do they know how to share their faith stories?
- Because evangelism starts with a relationship and kids understand God's message in stages, how are the people in your team building in those relationships so there is "skin" to Jesus?
- How are you passing on the vision to children's groups and adult groups?

SKILL DEVELOPMENT

- What skill do I need to help you with?
- What are two successes you've experienced this past month?
- What ministry struggles are you having? Do these struggles have anything in common?
- What is your priority for this month and why?
- How accurate is your job description for your job this month?
- How are you balancing team-building vs. ministry as a team?

TRAINING

- What specific training or skills have been taught and caught by your team members?
- What training needs do you have for yourself? For your team members?

MINISTRY MODELING

- What can I model in ministry for you?
- How are you modeling the vision and values of children's ministry within your team?
- Is prayer a priority or way of life for your team, or an afterthought?
- How is your pace? Are you tired? What are your expectations of yourself?
- What are your expectations of your lead teachers this month?
- How are you modeling the vision or awareness of adult recruitment in your team?

When you spend time developing your leaders, you'll find your ministry increases in effectiveness and vitality. As current leaders rise to the challenges you set before them, new leaders will emerge as other team members come alongside to share the load. And that's what the team approach to ministry is all about—sharing the load. Sharing the joys, sharing the struggles, sharing the failures and successes.

The team approach to ministry takes time, but it's worth it, because there's no way you can genuinely minister to all your volunteers apart from a team structure. Keith Johnson says, "If Jesus didn't spend time with twelve people, including a 'Judas,' where would Christianity be today?...Look at the benefit of being a developer of people whom you'll spend an eternity with."

"Team ministry is about creating a culture of care for each other," Keith continues. "Team ministry is the only way to delegate. Delegation is the only way to have a broad impact. Having a broad impact will translate into providing value to your church, your community, and your God."

Go, team!

In the New International Version Bible, there are fifty-six verses in the New Testament that mention Christians' responsibilities to "one another." On your own or with your team, evaluate your ministry by a sampling of these "one another" verses found in the New Testament:

- John 13:34-35;
- Romans 12:10; 12:16; 14:13; 15:7; 15:14;
- 1 Corinthians 11:33;
- Galatians 5:13; 6:1-2;
- Ephesians 4:2; 4:32; 5:21;
- Colossians 3:9; 3:13; 3:16;
- 1 Thessalonians 3:12; 5:11;
- Hebrews 3:13;
- James 5:16;
- 1 Peter 1:22; 4:8-10; 5:5; and
- 1 John 4:12.

A HEART FOR TEAMWORK

Darlene Pinson, children's director at Olive Baptist Church in Pensacola, Florida, oversees two hundred volunteers. You'll see Darlene's heart for teamwork in her responses to my questions.

Q: How have you "given away" ministry to volunteers for them to minister to each other?

A: In a team concept, one person cannot, and should not, do it all. Volunteers help minister to each other by home visits, phone contacts, and special occasion cards. They make visits to children in their departments and to prospects. Volunteers participate in the planning and leading of meetings for leadership.

Q: Why have you placed such a high priority on relationship-building?

A: That's the model Jesus gave. It builds fellowship and trust. It is a must for support during good times, as well as "trying" times.

Q: How do you make time for all the relational things you do with people with all the big-picture demands you have?

A: Much of the time, I don't feel like I do nearly enough in this area. However, this is always time well spent. It is money in the bank! For every attempt at being involved in the lives of volunteers and their families, there are countless rewards. The little things really do make a difference—a note, small gift, food, phone call, hospital or home visit—no matter what, just so they know they are special people who are cared about far more than just what they do as volunteers in children's ministry.

Q: How have you made volunteering worth people's time?

A: Keep the goals ever before them. They're every bit as much a minister as the professional minister. Theirs is kingdom work, with eternal rewards. They are not working for me, or for the church; they are serving their Lord in obedience and according (hopefully!) to their giftedness. In practical ways, it's necessary to provide supplies and equipment as needed. Affirm, acknowledge, support, and recognize them. Know them personally, and let them know you intimately also. Spend time and money on volunteer training. Keep up with training and learning for yourself, too. Learn from each other. Ask for, accept, and use their suggestions. Be available to them.

Q: What would you say to a children's minister who said, "I don't have time to build relationships with people; there are too many programs to get organized!"

A: A minister with that attitude probably won't stay in the work very long. We are PEOPLE, not programs. Programs are only a means to an end. Healthy relationships with volunteers will energize them to run the programs. A good leader will nurture and equip the people so they "partner" with you to do the work.

Chapter 5

SHEPHERDING VOLUNTEERS

When they had finished eating, Jesus said to Simon Peter, "Simon son of John, do you truly love me more than these?"

"Yes, Lord," he said, "you know that I love you."

Jesus said, "Feed my lambs."

Again Jesus said, "Simon son of John, do you truly love me?"

He answered, "Yes, Lord, you know that I love you."

Jesus said, "Take care of my sheep."

The third time he said to him, "Simon son of John, do you love me?"

Peter was hurt because Jesus asked him the third time, "Do you love me?" He said, "Lord, you know all things; you know that I love you."

Jesus said, "Feed my sheep."

—John 21:15-17

In Matthew 2:6, we're told that Jesus would shepherd his people. In the above passage, Jesus asked Peter three times, "Peter do you love me?" Each time Peter answered, he affirmed his love for Jesus. In response, Jesus told Peter "feed my lambs," "take care of my sheep," and "feed my sheep." The shepherding ministry is a direct commission from the Good Shepherd.

God gives "sheep" or people to servant leaders who desire a shepherding ministry. A shepherd's responsibility is to see that the people in his "flock" are fed, protected, guided, loved, and helped to mature and have a fruitful ministry. Sheep with a willing shepherd have fulfilling and productive lives and ministries.

But sheep without a shepherd are scattered and may lose their lives. Ezekiel 34:1-10 tells how God will deal with shepherds who don't shepherd their sheep. To the shepherd who doesn't care for the flock, God says, "This is what the Sovereign Lord says: I am against the shepherds and will hold them accountable for my flock. I will remove them from tending the flock so that the shepherds can no longer feed themselves. I will rescue my flock from their mouths, and it will no longer be food for them" (Ezekiel 34:10). In other words, if a shepherd neglects to care for his or her sheep, God will take away that shepherd's ministry.

God wants us to lead our flock—the children and staff in our children's ministry—into rest. We are to refresh and care for the people God has given us. But how can we do this with so many people—and still manage all our additional responsibilities on top of volunteer management? We have to admit that we can't do it all and we need help.

According to Darlene Pinson, children's director at Olive Baptist Church in Pensacola, Florida, and overseer of two hundred volunteers, a shepherding approach to children's ministry takes a special kind of manager who can share the ministry with volunteers. "It takes one who realizes their limitations, and understands that the joys and blessings of ministry are to be shared in order to create a ripple effect," she says. "Those who care to be known as a workaholic will not do this. Insecure and/or egotistical individuals refuse to delegate or to be a team player."

Hmm...Not a workaholic. Recognizes his or her limitations. Even if we do understand our limitations, it may seem more expedient for some people to carry the lion's share of the work themselves. It's just easier, they reason. "By doing it myself, I know it's done right and done on time," they rationalize. True enough. But to avoid burning ourselves out and to effectively shepherd our volunteers, we need to use a new ministry management model. We must share the load. Children's ministry shepherds must develop undershepherds who help oversee, support, motivate, encourage, and train people.

Judy Williamson, director of children's ministries at St. John's United Methodist Church in Albuquerque, New Mexico, says, "It's a challenge to keep my energy level high and have a day off from work. Our various children's programs are scheduled seven days from 7:30 a.m. until 8:30 p.m., plus child care for events lasting later for adults."

Judy oversees five hundred volunteers in a church of eighteen hundred. "I've overcome this challenge," she says, "by training volunteers not to expect me to be present at each event on two campuses. I'm encouraging volunteers to be in ministry to others rather than to expect me to do all the ministering."

Stop & Consider Read John 10:1-30. List the things that shepherds do for their sheep. Then list specific ways you can do these things for your volunteers.

SHEPHERDING THROUGH TEAMS

As a volunteer manager in children's ministry, your goal is to develop an effective ministry to children through volunteers. And it's a reciprocal venture. The way you recruit and manage volunteers has a direct influence on the way volunteers minister to children. If you invite volunteers into a relational ministry, they in turn will enter into a relational ministry with children. If you treat volunteers as projects to fill holes in a task-oriented ministry, they'll likely treat the children in your church the same way.

The shepherding approach to volunteer management is structured for such relational ties. No more are teachers handed their curriculum, led to their room, and left to their own devices until the next recruiting phase. Instead, volunteers are nurtured, motivated, encouraged and equipped as fully-functioning, valued team members.

Several years ago, I was on the staff of a Christian organization that worked with college students. Thinking that I needed a change of pace on Sunday mornings, I volunteered to teach the junior high class at my church. The class consisted of only four boys—three from the same home-schooled family. The Sunday school superintendent gave me my curriculum, pointed me to the room, and disappeared. I never saw another adult again during the Sunday school hour.

When it was time to sign up again, what do you think I did? That's right. I ran screaming into the night! OK, maybe teaching those junior high boys wasn't quite that bad, but I didn't sign up again. And the truth is: I felt like a failure. I didn't understand that it was the lack of teamwork, training, and support that made me not want to teach that class again. I thought I had a problem with commitment.

When I walked away from that class, I had no connections in the Sunday school program apart from the students in my class. Had I been part of a team that provided me with friendship, support, encouragement, and accountability, I might've had a more enjoyable—and long-term—experience.

Churches of all sizes understand this and are structuring their ministries into shepherding teams. The children's minister directly shepherds team leaders, or "undershepherds," who then shepherd the volunteers on their teams. For example, Debbie Neufeld, children's minister at Grant Memorial Baptist Church in Winnipeg, Manitoba, oversees 150 volunteers. She says, "I recruit team leaders for each age group and hour. They oversee their departments that include our core group leaders who work directly with the children."

Shepherding Volunteers

Debbie Wiesen, the children's minister at Spokane Valley Nazarene Church in Spokane, Washington, oversees sixty volunteers. She too has developed an undershepherd team structure in her ministry.

"I have three coordinators who oversee 2-4, K-3, and 4-6," Debbie says. "They help recruit teachers and find all the substitutes. I continue to train and nurture because all the coordinators work full-time."

Judy Basye, children's pastor at First Baptist of San Mateo, California, oversees 263 volunteers in a church with four hundred members. (Wow! Judy has over 50 percent of her church volunteering in children's ministry!) Like Debbie Neufeld and Debbie Wiesen, Judy uses an undershepherd approach to volunteer management.

In fact, most of the ministries highlighted or mentioned in this book have implemented Jesus' shepherding approach to volunteer management—and report tremendous results! The "Organize Your Team!" box (p. 49) illustrates how two dynamic children's ministries manage their volunteers.

Dwight Mix, children's pastor at Fellowship Bible Church in Lowell, Arkansas, manages 250 volunteers who minister to seven hundred kids. They've also organized according to an undershepherd approach. "This schematic fits us pretty closely," says Dwight. "However, we're constantly evaluating how we can improve and no doubt this structure will change. We're structured so we can focus more on meeting the needs of our volunteers—not just the teaching needs either."

"This year we changed two of our staff members' job descriptions to cause them to primarily focus on people," Dwight continues. "One person's job title is Leadership Relations Director and all she does is spend time relating to volunteers on a personal level. The other person is our Personnel Director, and her primary focus is training and equipping volunteers."

Having specialized paid staff members is usually a big church luxury, but there's no reason any size church can't structure its volunteer teams in the same ways that these churches have. But before you rush out to implement an undershepherd approach in your church, you'll need to consider these six components of team management: motivation, communication, empowerment, support, accountability, and celebration.

┌─ Quote ─┐

"Of all the things I've done, the most vital is coordinating the talents of those who work for us and pointing them toward a certain goal."

—Walt Disney

Organize Your Team!

Steven Wood, minister of Christian education at Westwood Church in Evansville, Indiana, has almost as many volunteers as he has children in his ministry. He manages 125 volunteers who minister to 150 kids. Here's Steven's schematic:

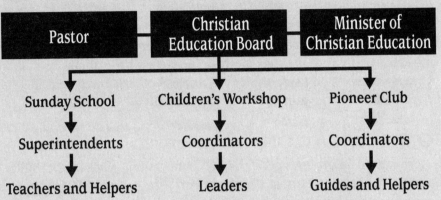

Dann Lies, children's pastor at Living Word Christian Center in Brooklyn Park, Minnesota, manages 250 volunteers who minister to 425 children. Here's Dann's schematic:

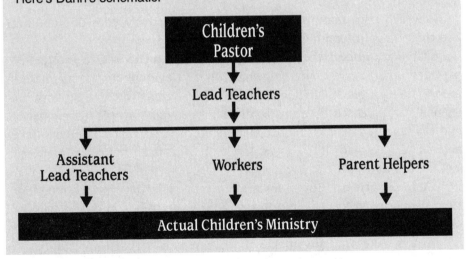

MOTIVATION

In the area of motivation, let Barnabas be your example. The name Barnabas means "encourager." Barnabas was a mentor, encourager, and shepherd for many of the leaders in the young Christian church. Barnabas consistently gave to meet needs (Acts 4:36-37), believed in others (Acts 9:26-31), and built up the church (Acts 11:22-26).

People thrive on encouragement, so it's generally best to interact with volunteers using a 90/10 rule: Give 90 percent encouragement and 10 percent correction. Sometimes it's hard to encourage when you really feel like correcting. Just ask Robbie Joshua, children's pastor at Faith Community Church in West Covina, California. Robbie says, "I've had to train myself to be an encourager, even when I don't feel like it. From my perspective, the glass has to be 'half full rather than half empty.' "

As you look for ways to encourage your volunteers in ministry, ask God to show you their spiritual gifts. Your volunteers find great fulfillment in using their God-given gifts, so motivate and encourage them by pointing out ways you see God using their gifts to bless others. For a helpful guide, see Appendix 4: "Motivating Through Gifts" (p. 123).

COMMUNICATION

"What binds a group together is communication," says Harold Bullock, senior pastor at Hope Baptist Church in Fort Worth, Texas. "If communication breaks down, the group falls apart."

Robbie Joshua agrees. She says, "Because of our team ministry, I've had to develop systems of communication to keep my 'finger on the pulse' of hundreds of people."

How can your team communicate more effectively with one another? Use these keys to communication.

● **Give advanced notice to key leaders and the entire group.** People need time to adopt anything that'll mean personal cost or sacrifice in money, time, or effort. Advanced notice allows teams to come up with better plans and ideas. It develops leadership by helping people learn, analyze, and evaluate. It produces higher ownership of ideas that volunteers know about and have had time to give input on. Advanced notice helps people feel needed and in the know.

● **Use repetition.** Communication is made effective through repetition. Most people need to hear information four to six times in order to understand and recall it. So keep the communication flowing!

Always take full advantage of written and verbal opportunities to communicate with your volunteers. In addition to fliers, postcards, and posters, try sending your volunteers a quarterly calendar or newsletter with standard and special meetings or programs they're required to attend. Use fun clip-art books to dress up your calendars, such as the *Kids' Worker's Clip Art Book* from Gospel Light (1-800-235-3415) or *Children's Ministry Clip Art* from Group Publishing, Inc., (1-800-447-1070).

Verbal communication with volunteers is important, but can also be time-consuming, especially in a large church. If you find yourself spending much of your time on the phone with volunteers, check out PhoneTree. This electronic device can call and deliver messages to over nine hundred people at a time. The people who are called can also leave simple responses, such as pressing 1 if they plan to attend or 2 if they don't. PhoneTree is available from Personal Communication Systems for $499. Call 1-800-951-8733.

● **Create a handbook.** Having a children's ministry handbook facilitates communication and clarifies policies for your volunteers. Custom-make your handbook to include these components and more:
  ● your children's ministry's philosophy,
  ● church and children's ministry policies and procedures,
  ● location of materials,
  ● discipline philosophy,
  ● contact people and phone numbers,
  ● typical behavior and other age-level expectations,
  ● abuse prevention policies,
  ● teacher expectations,
  ● training times and locations,
  ● team meetings,
  ● sample postcards to send to children,
  ● class rosters with listed addresses and birthdays, and
  ● specific articles to read.
Share your notebook with your volunteers in a training meeting or individually. Have all your volunteers sign a form stating that they've read and understand church policies as stated in the notebook. File this form in your office.

EMPOWERMENT

Jesus-style leadership requires promoting other people into places where they shine. Before Jesus went back to heaven, he empowered his volunteer disciples to carry on his work. "All authority in heaven and on earth has been given to me," Jesus said, "Therefore go and make disciples of all nations, baptizing them in the name of the Father and of the Son and of the Holy Spirit, and teaching them to obey everything I have commanded you" (Matthew 28:18-20).

Jesus shared his authority. Have you? Letting go and empowering volunteers can be difficult, because it involves giving up control. "How can I let other people run ministries?" many children's ministers wonder. "Their work may not be as good as what I would do. Or, even worse, maybe it'll be better than what I would do and then I'll look bad either way," they think.

"The biggest problem with a discipleship approach to volunteer management is the leader," says Lon W. Flippo, a children's ministry consultant from the Assemblies of God church in Springfield, Missouri. "If the leader is bound up by pride and control, he's going to have a hard time letting go and allowing teams to be empowered and released."

If you struggle with such things, I have only one thing to say to you—be healed of that unheavenly attitude! Alan E. Nelson writes in *Leading Your Ministry,* "The world applauds the person who can take control...But the way of the cross is giving up control to God."

Effective volunteer managers must give up control and delegate meaningful responsibilities to volunteers. Says Robbie Joshua, "I've had to learn to 'give away' parts of the ministry to facilitate growth and momentum in the team, even when I've felt that I could do it better and quicker. Because I tend to be a detail-oriented person (and can easily get caught up in 'micro-managing'), I'm constantly challenged to keep a global perspective."

Part of having a "global perspective" is having a vision for how people will grow as they're trusted with challenging tasks that you'll enable them to succeed in. A good business executive picks out possible successors and trains them in significant parts of the executive's job. In addition to strengthening your ministry team, delegation allows you to train your replacement should you ever leave (or get sick, or be called away for an extended period of time).

When you delegate, you not only develop leaders, but you also discover them. Darrell Fraley, children's pastor at Hope Church in Cincinnati, Ohio, says he's in the business of training children's pastors. "You can't go anywhere with the uncommitted. You have to focus on those who are movin' and shakin,' " Darrell says. "Cream always rises to the top. Those who are committed show up when they say they will and they stay late to complete the job. Locating future children's pastors is like 'survival of the fittest.' The ones who keep going, stay faithful, hang in there, and don't quit are the ones who have the potential of doing the job of a children's pastor."

Follow these guidelines to good delegation:

1. Overcome your reasons for not delegating. The top obstacles to delegation are:

> ┌ *Quote* ┐
>
> "It's amazing what can be accomplished if you don't worry about who gets the credit."
>
> —Clarence W. Jones

- fear that the person may not follow through,
- anxiety that the delegated task may not be "excellent" enough,
- procrastinating and not allowing enough time to delegate,
- laziness (it's easier to do a task yourself than to hassle with delegating),
- a fear of supervisors thinking you're not doing enough if you don't do everything, and
- not wanting to bother people or impose.

2. Determine what you should and should not delegate. Always delegate these things: things others can do; things that are not priority items for you; things you cannot do well; and things that'll develop or stretch others.

3. Make sure volunteers know the ball is theirs. Don't micromanage. The leader who tells volunteers what to do and exactly how to do it is guilty of over-managing. Don't rob volunteers of the thrill of using their brains, resources, and creativity. Instead, manage by objectives. Tell volunteers the results you want, and let them figure out for themselves how they'll get the job done.

4. Give volunteers a clear job description. Writing out job descriptions triples their effectiveness. Provide parameters such as budget, quality standards, and theme for each delegated task. Tell volunteers what, when, and why you want something done. Don't just focus on the task and say, "We need you to decorate for our Valentine's Day party." Instead, motivate people with the greater vision by giving instructions such as "Your job is to decorate the fellowship hall for our Valentine's Day party so kids will sense in a new way how much God loves them."

5. Give volunteers the authority to carry out the task. Clearly define which decisions are within the volunteer's jurisdiction and which decisions require consultation with you or someone else.

6. Monitor the delegated task. People need reminders. So flag your calendar with periodic check-back dates when you'll talk with volunteers just to see how the task is going and if there's anything you can do to help. Give direction as needed. If volunteers hit snags, think through solutions to problems. Help them be faithful and successful.

- **Support.** "Since volunteers leave their adult class to serve in the children's area, my greatest challenge is to provide support to them personally and to minister to their needs," says Cynthia Petty.

Paul Colomy, Huey-tsyh Chen, and Gregg Andrews, authors of "Situational Facilities and Volunteer Work" (as excerpted from *Secrets of Motivation* by Sue Vineyard), discovered that three of the top five reasons 300 volunteers gave for job satisfaction are people-related. Volunteers are looking for the opportunity to help people; and they want a competent supervisor who'll support them.

The night before my first Sunday morning teacher-enrichment meetings, I was anxious about all the logistics. So when one of the Christian Education Board members, Ellie Case, called me, I felt tremendous support. "Chris, this is Ellie," she said. "Steve and I are at the church and we just wondered if there's anyway we can help you get ready for tomorrow." Wow! And then in the morning, Ellie checked with me again and asked me if anyone had prayed with me yet about the meetings. She held my hands and sweetly prayed for me. I remember thinking, "Who *wouldn't* want to volunteer here with this kind of support!"

The greatest support you can give your volunteers is to understand their situations and constraints. If you and your children's ministry team support a volunteer when life comes tumbling down, your entire team is strengthened.

Cheryl Hall, children's pastor at East Tulsa Christian Church in Tulsa, Oklahoma, describes her volunteer team. "We're like a family. When one of us hurts, we all hurt. We simply just care about each other. Last year, one of our preschool teachers was also the janitor of our church. Her husband became very ill. Our volunteers took food in. They cleaned the building. They made sure the janitorial duties were covered. Let me tell you—that's a labor of love."

Other practical ways you can provide support to your volunteers:

• **Encourage spiritual growth.** Tammy Ross, director of preschool ministries at First Baptist Church in Columbia, Tennessee, says, "Several years ago we began a teacher Bible study on Tuesday mornings through fall and spring. We usually do a study that's twelve to fourteen weeks long. We also do more teacher fellowships to include those who work and can't be a part of the study."

Provide your volunteers with daily devotion books, sermon cassettes, and suggested Bible readings. Encourage them to have a daily devotion time. Periodically, ask them what they're learning in their personal time with God.

And while you're at it, don't forget to make time for your own personal growth. "I've had to learn to schedule my personal growth time," says Robbie Joshua, "which includes daily 'quiet time' with God, reading good books, and spending time with quality people who mentor and challenge me to grow." What's good for the sheep is also good for the shepherd!

• **Provide easy and effective resources.** Andrea Shintaku, a teacher in the musical theater program at Community Church of Joy in Glendale, Arizona, says, "What's really good is that our leaders try to provide us with a really good curriculum. I only have forty-five minutes and usually there's five or six things to choose from and tailor-make it for your class and still get the point across of what the lesson is supposed to be."

● **Set up a teachers lounge for volunteers to use whenever they're serving.** A teacher's lounge doesn't have to be fancy or spacious. But volunteers sometimes need a place to get away and relax or visit with each other. Always provide a bountiful supply of refreshments.

● **Establish a parent helper room where parents can drop in to complete projects for volunteers.** Put a deadline on each project so helpers will know when to complete them. Have parent helpers sign in so you can keep track of their help—and affirm and recognize their service.

● **Create a resource room.** LuAnn Robinson, the fifth-grade Sunday school teacher at Whittier Hills Baptist Church in La Habra, California, says, "When our church started a resource room, it was a major help. I felt like somebody really cared. I could give them a list of supplies I needed ahead of time or go in at the last minute and find cotton balls or straws. The other thing that's helpful since I work full time is that I can use the resource room's photocopier at anytime. They gave all the teachers a key to the resource center so I can make copies, get poster board and paints, or use the hole punchers at any time of the day. This is really a plus for me!"

ACCOUNTABILITY

A successful volunteer manager gives feedback to volunteers on a regular and expected basis. Build into volunteers' job descriptions at every level when and how reviews or evaluations will be conducted.

Volunteer evaluations can be as simple as a classroom observation with 90 percent affirmation and 10 percent correction. Or perhaps you'll get feedback from a volunteer coordinator's team and meet with the coordinator to go over the feedback. How often you conduct these reviews is up to you, but they should happen at least once during a volunteer's term of service—and more often if there are problems you're trying to remedy through the accountability process, such as helping the volunteer maintain better classroom management.

Another crucial learning opportunity that many volunteer managers fail to capitalize on is conducting "exit interviews" with volunteers who resign. Businesses do this on a regular basis to try to discover how they can strengthen their company and employee relations. If you learn why volunteers are leaving, you may discover trends that point to areas of need in your volunteer management style.

It's a tricky thing to conduct an exit interview because people aren't always clear on why they no longer want to volunteer. But with prayer and loving probing, you can discover the real reasons. As I researched this book, I talked to many volunteers who've recently resigned from children's ministry. Some of these people had straightforward answers, such as having a baby or medical problems. Others gave reasons such as being too busy or choosing something else instead of children's ministry. It's these reasons

TELL ME MORE

To help you understand the process of conducting exit interviews with volunteers, here's a record of one "exit interview" I conducted with a volunteer who'd recently resigned.

Q: Why did you resign from children's ministry?

A: Really the only reason that I didn't want to do it this year was because I wanted to go to a women's class. They were doing a Bible study.

Q: It sounds like you may've been looking for teaching and relationships with women. Do you think there's anything your volunteer coordinator could've done to meet those needs for you?

A: No, not really. They offered options, but I couldn't go.

Q: What is it that attracted you to the study?

A: It's interesting to me and different from what I'm doing.

Q: It sounds like it met a real felt need for you.

A: Yeah.

Q: 'Cause you made a choice. I'd like to understand why one choice was more appealing than the other.

A: OK, I'll tell you for my particular class why I didn't want to go back and teach two-year-olds.

Q: OK.

A: Um. These particular teachers had taught this class for a while, and there wasn't a lot of teaching going on. I struggled with it every Sunday. I feel like these kids come to Sunday school for Bible teaching and not just babysitting. A lot of it was playtime, and there was no discipline. I was the one putting the child in time-out and that wasn't favorably received sometimes. And I think chaos reigns if you let it. So in that particular class I really struggled because these teachers were there and they had been there and been there and been there and it was their class.

Q: You didn't feel like you had much "say."

A: No, and my daughter was in the class and I was distressed because I could see no teaching going on. It was a frustrating year for me.

that merit further probing. See the "Tell Me More" box (p. 56) to learn how you can get the real scoop.

Exit interviews can unearth all kinds of helpful information! Because this particular volunteer was also a parent concerned about her daughter's learning, we can see that this two-year-old class needed to do more teaching. Although this church had just "lost" that volunteer, through an exit interview it could've gained valuable insights about an area of children's ministry that could be strengthened.

CELEBRATION

It's important to shine a light on all the good things that are happening in your volunteers' ministry. Your volunteers are idealistic people who want to make a difference in kids' lives. Help them see that they are.

Celebrating volunteers' efforts also has side-benefits for recruiting. As you publicly celebrate your children's ministry, potential volunteers see the excitement and thrill of being used by God to reach children. Celebration helps your church "fall in love with" the children of your church.

Steven Wood assertively publicizes his children's ministry to the five hundred people in his church. Because Steven visibly celebrates volunteers' work, volunteer retention is strengthened.

"The individuals on our ministry teams make one-year commitments, after which time they are free to move on if they feel led to," Steven says. "Because the congregation knows what's going on, the overwhelming majority of folks renew their commitments. I think this has a great deal to do with the fact that they feel like they're doing something important and were well-informed before they ever came on board."

There are many ways to make kids, volunteers, and your program more visible in your church. Steven shares a few:

● Print updates in the weekly church bulletin and monthly church newsletter.

● Take over the main bulletin board once in a while and post pictures of a recent children's event.

● Have your pastor announce children's ministry events and pray for your church's children's ministries.

● Present a quarterly video for the whole congregation that contains clips from various ministries.

● Put on a variety of special programs throughout the year, including children's choir musicals, Christmas programs, and the VBS closing program.

Celebrate your volunteers, and your church will celebrate with you!

TROUBLESHOOTING

Wouldn't it be great if managing volunteers was a wholly positive experience? Unfortunately, thanks to human nature (including our own!), problems with volunteers do tend to pop up from time to time. Here are six possible management problems and suggestions for dealing with each one. As always when dealing with a tough situation, the first step you need to take is to ask God for wisdom.

1. Wrong match. After you've placed a volunteer in a position, she may tell you that "things aren't working out; it just wasn't a good match." To solve the case of the mismatched volunteer, follow these steps:

● **Listen.** Get the volunteer's perspective. Ask, "Why do you think this isn't a good match? How have you felt in your ministry role? What specific things have been the most frustrating to you?"

● **Observe the volunteer in his or her ministry.** Perhaps there are other factors that if dealt with would alleviate the problem. Determine if additional help, training, or resources would help ease the volunteer's frustration.

Because of discipline challenges in their classrooms, Debbie Wiesen says, "We've added additional helpers in every department. That's made a huge difference. We're writing and teaching a four-week program about respect of self, others, God, and the church building."

● **If the volunteer and ministry position truly have been mismatched, meet with the volunteer and discuss your observations.** Affirm the volunteer's contribution and value to your children's ministry team. Say, "You're such a valuable team member that we don't want to lose you. Here are other areas in our ministry that you may enjoy serving in more. Why don't we pray and ask God to point out where he would like you to serve? Let's get together next week to talk about this."

● **Monitor the volunteer.** If the volunteer chooses a new role, check back weekly during the first month to see how it's going. Then check back monthly for the next three months. If no problems arise, you most likely have a good match.

● **Accept a final resignation as final.** If the volunteer decides to resign completely from children's ministry, graciously thank her for her service and positively communicate to the rest of your team that God has led this volunteer in a different direction.

2. Personal crisis. When you're aware that a volunteer is facing a personal crisis, don't wait for him to come to you. Offer your support. Ask what you can do to help in the situation. Ask, "How can I assist you in your ministry to help you through this time?" Offer to provide extra helpers, a substitute for a brief sabbatical, or relief from entire duties. As you do this, you'll communicate to the volunteer that he is ever-so-much more valuable to you as a person than as a volunteer. And, most likely, he'll be back when his life evens out.

3. Poor performance. If a volunteer's nonmoral performance glitch is affecting her ability to minister to children, act quickly. For our purposes here, we'll use tardiness as an example. Follow these steps:

• Meet with the volunteer and get her perspective on the performance issue. Say, "I've been told that you've been fifteen minutes late to class the last three weeks. Is that true?"

• Explain why this is a concern to you. Say something such as, "I'm sure you understand that time with our children is precious and we have so little time with them on Sundays. How do you think your tardiness affects children?"

• Find out why the problem is occurring. Say, "I just wonder what's been going on since this hasn't been a problem in the past. Can we talk about it?"

Perhaps the volunteer will tell you that she's in the middle of a divorce and her husband gives her a hard time every time she tries to take the children to church. Or perhaps she's on a new medication that makes it difficult to awaken. On the other hand, she may tell you that she has lost interest in her class and just doesn't want to get up in the mornings.

• Discuss solutions to the problem so that children are best served. Determine a plan for remedying the problem and set up a period of time for things to improve. In your plan, list what the volunteer will do and what you'll do to correct the problem. (Perhaps you'll call her at 6 a.m. every Sunday to help her awaken.) Both of you sign and date the plan. File a copy of this plan in your office.

• Check back periodically to monitor progress. Meet with the volunteer at the end of the time period to determine if things have improved or if she may need to be reassigned to a position that would be unaffected by the problem—in this case, a position that doesn't require punctuality.

If you believe reassigning the volunteer to another position is only a bandage on a bigger problem, then you'll have to "fire" the volunteer. Explain to her that the quality of ministry to children cannot continue to be compromised. For the sake of the children in her class, tell the volunteer that she can no longer serve in this capacity.

4. Sexual misconduct. The best defense is a good offense, so hopefully you've adequately screened the volunteer (see page 72 for more information on screening volunteers). If someone accuses a volunteer of any kind of sexual abuse, follow these steps from *Reducing the Risk of Child Sexual Abuse in Your Church* by Richard R. Hammar, Steven W. Klipowicz, and James F. Cobble, Jr:

1. Document all your efforts at handling the incident.

2. Report the incident immediately to your church leadership, church insurance company, attorney, and denominational officials.

3. Contact the proper civil authorities. Involve your attorney in any interviews with police. Don't attempt to conduct an investigation on your own. Leave this to the professionals who are familiar with these cases.

4. Notify the parents.

5. Secure the safety of the child. Show care and support to the victim and the victim's family.

6. Do not prejudge the situation, but take the allegations seriously and reach out to the victim and the victim's family.

7. Treat the accused with dignity and support. That person should be relieved temporarily of his or her duties until the investigation is finished.

8. Respond to the press with written prepared public statements, if necessary. Safeguard the privacy and confidentiality of all involved.

5. Unstaffed class on Sunday morning. You have two choices if children arrive and adult volunteers don't. Behind door number one: Make an emergency plea from the pulpit for someone—anyone—to come help. Behind door number two: Shut down the class, and say, "I'm sorry, we don't have staff to provide this class to your children today. They'll have to go to class (or worship) with you."

I choose door number two, Monty.

Why? Making a desperate plea for volunteers is high-risk because you could just get the "anyone" that no one would've ever chosen through an appropriate screening process. Further, you've telegraphed to your entire congregation that children's ministry is a desperate, hobbling program rather than the exciting place where children meet their Savior.

If you don't shut down the program, you risk creating a dysfunctional congregation with you as its primary co-dependent trying to cover for its irresponsibility and lack of commitment. Ouch! Rather than try to cover up the problem, reveal it and allow God to work in the hearts of people to call them to this ministry.

Michaele Rhodes, a previous volunteer at First Baptist Church in Columbia, Tennessee, says that she specifically volunteered in children's ministry because "the most effective way I've ever been recruited is when I realized that some of my kids weren't going to have teachers because they couldn't get enough."

6. Uncooperative teachers. Darrell Fraley says his greatest challenge is "volunteers from the previous children's ministry director who aren't able to (or can't) make adjustments or changes to new systems or growth very well."

Robbie Joshua has dealt with the same problem. "Whenever I've encountered resistance to this organizational setup," she says, "I can usually trace it to one of three things: a lack of loyalty (to the vision or myself as the leader); a lack of ability that causes feelings of insecurity; or a lack of maturity (either spiritually or emotionally)."

"Whenever this has occurred, I've approached these people in love and tried to clarify our vision and their unique contribution to its success. I look for an opportunity to redirect them to a place on the team where they can be successful," Robbie continues. "However, I do firmly believe that it's important, as coach of this team, to remove (always in love) anyone who refuses to be a team player, and I have done so when a resistant person has negatively affected the climate or momentum of the team. When serving God's kids, our personal agendas have to take a back seat to the bigger purposes."

Philippians 2:1-4 says, "If you have any encouragement from being united with Christ, if any comfort from his love, if any fellowship with the Spirit, if any tenderness and compassion, then make my joy complete by being like-minded, having the same love, being one in spirit and purpose. Do nothing out of selfish ambition or vain conceit, but in humility consider others better than yourselves. Each of you should look not only to your own interests, but also to the interests of others." As always, Jesus is our example, and his humility is what we should strive for in ourselves and model for our volunteers as we shepherd them in ministry.

SHEPHERDING THROUGH TEAMS

Keith Johnson, pastor to children at Wooddale Church in Eden Prairie, Minnesota, explains how he shepherds his volunteer teams.

● **Team structure.** "Our children's ministry team consists of several layers. First there is the Associates who are paid to work twenty hours a week. Next are the Coordinators who oversee roughly the same age span (two grades or ages) that the Associates do but are not paid for it. We meet together once a month to coordinate the total program and to assess needs and go through names to recruit from. I personally meet with these 'undershepherds' weekly either by phone (Coordinators) or in a formal meeting (Associates). This ministry team structure allows for a group of key volunteers to carry out the ministry they feel strongly about.

"I've learned a lot about myself in this team process. I regularly get feedback that is both highly negative and highly positive. That comes with the territory. Because the team approach is more 'other' centered, it has been difficult because I have a natural self-centeredness. I have learned that I can learn from people who don't agree with me…that the healthiest groups avoid homogeneity (same age, same gender, and socioeconomic status)…and that I can have a cranky naysayer and we can still grow as a group.

● **Advantages.** "First, team-shepherding creates a buffer zone. The space between those who work directly with children and their leader gives great comfort and security to those in the trenches. They have an advocate, someone they can cry to and someone who meets their needs.

"Second, it produces community. Connected volunteers feel the pressure of a group if they fail to show up. If a disinterested 'recruiter' has merely placed someone in a room all by himself, chances are he won't last nor will he feel supported.

"Third, it fulfills the biblical mandate to 'equip the saints for works of service.' Paul's advice to the church in Ephesus was not to have a few do the work but for a few leaders to equip, train, and encourage others to fulfill their own mission and purpose.

"Workers are retained simply because they feel like they are part of a community, a mini-church if you will. They are supported and identify with others who struggle and succeed together."

● **Disadvantages.** "First, it takes time. It is a time-consuming task to develop another person. But discipleship isn't easy; Christianity is a process that is best modeled with leaders who teach it to others.

"Second, it requires a leader to be there. My staff stresses out when I am not in town. Voice mail is awkward and does not communicate because there is no shared meaning and misunderstandings can occur.

"Third, key leaders can disappoint. They can move away, resign because of pregnancy, or just lose interest. Because you have invested so much energy in them, this can be personally devastating.

"Fourth, it requires everyone to be heading in the same direction. It's a dysfunctional situation when one person just doesn't fit the team. Unity is a biblical sign of maturity, but it takes work (Ephesians 4:3-4, 11-16).

● **Obstacles.** "The reasons people resist a team are as varied as people themselves. First, it could be that the person has been burned before by 'relying' on a team. They figure that doing it themselves is easier and therefore better.

"Second, people lose control and power when they become part of a team. They must subject their ideas to the scrutiny and judgment of a group and that can be threatening.

"Third, people resist a team approach to ministry because they have never done it that way. Maybe they are in a job where they do not have to think, and are merely told what to do. They take that to church and it becomes a robotic way to minister, efficient but void of life-giving enthusiasm or originality.

"Fourth, people sometimes just cannot get along with one another. It becomes a dysfunctional family where honesty and openness are not valued.

"You overcome all of these things by starting with your core team and showing others what success looks like. That's vision. People fear what they don't know. Show them what it looks like and how it benefits them and they will help you out immensely!"

CASTING THE NET

As he approached Bethphage and Bethany at the hill called the Mount of Olives, he sent two of his disciples, saying to them, "Go to the village ahead of you, and as you enter it, you will find a colt tied there, which no one has ever ridden. Untie it and bring it here. If anyone asks you, 'Why are you untying it?' tell him, 'The Lord needs it.' "

Those who were sent ahead went and found it just as he had told them. As they were untying the colt, its owners asked them, "Why are you untying the colt?"

They replied, "The Lord needs it."

They brought it to Jesus, threw their cloaks on the colt and put Jesus on it.

—Luke 19:29-35

H ere's a behind-the-scenes story I'd love to know more about. Before the disciples ever arrived, what happened in the hearts of the colt's owners? How were they able to make such a sacrifice? How did Jesus prepare them to be ready for service? Wouldn't it be great if recruiting were that easy?

That's just it; it is! Or it can be.

Over and over in the Bible, we see stories of God's miraculous provision for his servants once they were commissioned to do God's work. Noah had everything he needed to build the ark; Solomon had everything he needed to build the temple; Nehemiah had everything he needed to rebuild the walls of Jerusalem. Just as the disciples had more than enough fish when they cast their nets in obedience to Jesus, you have everything you need to build a children's ministry.

Scripture is filled with admonitions for us to trust God to do the work that he has put in our hearts. In fact, it's very clear that it's impossible to carry out God's work without God's help. Throughout Scripture, God's servants are warned not to put their faith in people, resources, or methods other than God's miraculous provision. Consider these verses:

May he give you the desire of your heart and make all your plans succeed. We will shout for joy when you are victorious and will lift up our banners in the name of our God. May the Lord grant all your requests. Now I know that the Lord saves his anointed; he answers him from his holy heaven with the saving power of his right hand. Some trust in chariots and some in horses, but we trust in the name of the Lord our God.

—Psalm 20:4-7

Unless the Lord builds the house, its builders labor in vain. Unless the Lord watches over the city, the watchmen stand guard in vain. In vain you rise early and stay up late, toiling for food to eat—for he grants sleep to those he loves.

—Psalm 127:1-2

"Woe to the obstinate children," declares the Lord, "to those who carry out plans that are not mine, forming an alliance, but not by my Spirit, heaping sin upon sin; who go down to Egypt without consulting me; who look for help to Pharaoh's protection, to Egypt's shade for refuge. But Pharaoh's protection will be to your shame, Egypt's shade will bring you disgrace."

—Isaiah 30:1-3

Recruitment can be the most difficult and discouraging area of volunteer management—if we try to do it in our time and by our plans. But in God's time and by God's plan, it will be done. Perhaps in recruitment more than any other area of volunteer management, God wants to us to stand back and see his mighty hand. God wants to do the miraculous in calling out people to service.

The struggles of finding enough volunteers are nothing new. Jesus, himself, said in Luke 10:2, "The harvest is plentiful, but the workers are few. Ask the Lord of the harvest, therefore, to send out workers into his harvest field."

After Jesus pointed out that the workers are few, he didn't suggest new methods; he said to cry out to God. It's not a one-time, at-the-beginning-of-the-recruiting-phase prayer. It's the same kind of desperate, ongoing plea that Moses made to God when he prayed, "If you are pleased with me, teach me your ways so I may know you and continue to find favor with you...If your Presence does not go with us, do not send us up from here" (Exodus 33:13, 15). It's saying every step of the way, "I don't want to—I can't—do this without you, God."

"For many years volunteer recruitment was my greatest stumbling block in the ministry," says Clara

> **Quote**
>
> *"Usually when God is going to do a great work, I have noticed that there is a time of great dearth. Nothing moves. Nothing happens. All seems so stagnant. These are golden opportunities for prayer. Our Lord needs prayer, and keeps things from happening, to open space for Himself. And He is that satisfying portion we need—that food and drink is Himself."*
>
> —Joy Ridderhof

Olson, Family Life Pastor at New Hope Community Church in Portland, Oregon. "Today, I am happy to say, it is one of my greatest joys. What made the difference? God helped me to change my attitude and philosophy."

Because Clara recruits out of a sense of being God's talent scout, she has a low rate of volunteer turnover. "I believe that God cares about what's happening for kids," Clara says. "And I believe that he is calling people to work with them. I can be the audible voice. But if a person does not have a sense of God in this, then I don't want them with kids. There's not much heart in it. I have to ask myself, 'How can God bless that with real fruit?' You know, hearts that are changed, kids who really know the Lord?"

"I think recruiting volunteers and helping them to find a place to use the gifts that God has given them is the most exciting part of the job," Clara continues. "It's fun to see people suddenly experience success and know that their life has taken on purpose and meaning, and that they're working together with God to make a difference in the world."

The art of recruiting is listening to God's work in hearts and responding to the Spirit of God. It's tasting the miraculous evidence of our awesome God in the lives of his people.

In this book, we've already looked at principles of servant leadership from Jesus' life. We've walked through the process of creating a vision statement, and we've discovered the effectiveness of managing volunteers through shepherding teams. Understanding and applying everything we've explored thus far is the greatest path to retaining volunteers and reducing the constant turnover that leads to pressing recruiting needs. In this chapter, we'll examine recruiting strategies that will enable you to discover the people God has already selected for your children's ministry team and invite them to sign on.

SETTING THE STAGE

Before you ever approach a potential volunteer, you can organize your ministry to make the recruiting process more effective and ensure greater satisfaction for your volunteers. Here's how.

● **Know who's volunteering, and why.** It's not scientific, but according to my informal research, the two most common characteristics of people who volunteer are a servant's heart and a love for children. And the most common life factors of volunteers? The typical volunteer is married with young children at home and works outside the home.

From a more scientific study, it was revealed that approximately 50 percent of American adults volunteer regularly and slightly more than 50 percent of teenagers volunteer regularly. According to research conducted by the Gallup Organization concerning volunteering and philanthropy since 1980, people volunteer for six key reasons.

1. They want to do something useful. People want to make a difference and do something useful. George Kunzle, a former volunteer at Whittier Hills Baptist Church in LaHabra, California, tells why he first volunteered. "You hear stories now and again of kids who say, 'I took Christianity or Jesus Christ seriously just because of a teacher in such-a-such class in years gone by.' So you hope that you're going to make some kind of difference like that."

2. They think they'll enjoy the work. Most children's ministry volunteers just love kids! You can enhance your volunteers' natural enjoyment by matching them with an assignment they can excel at.

3. They think a friend or family member will benefit. People respond to requests to work in programs that help those they care about. Perhaps that's why most volunteers in Christian education programs are mothers of young children.

4. They've previously benefited from the activity. Self-help groups have been the fastest growing segment of volunteering today. If your church offers parenting classes, ask recent graduates to consider serving as future leaders. Inspire outstanding volunteers to even greater excellence by encouraging them to shepherd others as they've been mentored by you (as one of your "undershepherds").

5. They want to learn and get experience. People want to grow, understand and build skills. For example, new parents and young married couples may choose to volunteer in the nursery to help themselves become more comfortable around babies. Grandparents may volunteer in children's ministry to find out what today's kids are like.

6. They have lots of free time. And they want to fill that time with meaningful work. Retirees may want to use their skills from former careers. Lonely people want contact with others to form relationships.

(reasons excerpted from *Secrets of Motivation* by Sue Vineyard)

People are busy, but perhaps not as busy as they think. People will always make time for what they value in their lives. According to a "Time for Life" study by John Robinson and Geoffrey Godbey, adults average 39.4 hours free time per week, up from 34.8 hours in 1965. Here are the top five ways adults use that free time:

- Watch television—15 percent
- Socialize (visits, meals, parties)—6.7 percent

● **List all positions.** Create varied volunteer roles requiring either high- or low-level commitment. For example, a volunteer may not be able to commit to teaching an entire year, but he or she would be happy to coordinate the crafts or serve as a greeter one month out of each quarter. Instead of working in the nursery right away, perhaps new parents would rather help clean toys or wash crib linens. Take a close look at your programs, and you'll be surprised at the variety of roles you have available.

If you've never considered all the places volunteers can serve, consider these from Gordon and Becki West, children's ministry consultants in Mesa, Arizona:

● teacher
● substitute teacher
● greeter
● bulletin board aide
● decorator
● name tag maker
● parent helper
● party organizer
● music leader
● birthday card sender
● special events coordinator
● puppet team member

● lead teacher
● secretary
● snacks coordinator
● assistant anything
● curriculum manager
● closet organizer
● parent helper coordinator
● music coordinator
● prayer partner
● follow-up team member
● puppet team coordinator

These are just a few. As you can see, there's a place for anyone who wants to get involved at any level in children's ministry.

● **Crunch your numbers.** Take a look at all your programs and determine which positions are filled and which ones require more volunteers.

How many volunteers will you need? The first thing to consider is child-to-teacher ratios; you want to make sure that children are safe in your care. These are accepted worker-to-child ratios:

Nursery   1 adult to 3 children
Ages 2 to 3   1 adult to 4 children

Ages 4 to 5	1 adult to 5 children
1st and 2nd graders	1 adult to 6 children
3rd and 4th graders	1 adult to 7 children
5th and 6th graders	1 adult to 8 children

Beyond the ratios, consider the minimum number of volunteers you'll require in each room to ensure a safe environment for children. For the sake of children and adult volunteers, the absolute minimum is two adults per classroom. This two-adult rule protects children from a potential predator who might have opportunity to harm them without the presence of another volunteer. And it provides a corroborating witness for volunteers should there ever be a false accusation of abuse. I know of one nursery coordinator who requires three volunteers per classroom to ensure that there are always two volunteers in the room should one of the volunteers have to take a child to the restroom.

● **Determine the length of service for each position.** Not everyone wants to commit to a full-time ministry position. "We provide opportunities for serving part-time," Cynthia Petty of Lake Pointe Baptist Church in Rockwall, Texas, says. "Then we schedule and send reminder cards to our part-time people."

One of the most devastating practices we have in our churches today is the exclusive use of part-time teachers. I've been one—the teacher who shows up once a month or for a full month every quarter. And children call me "Teacher," because I'm never there long enough for them to learn my name.

When workers show up once a month (or, in a large church with many workers, possibly even less frequently) they never really get to know and love the children in their classrooms. There is no single volunteer in the classroom consistently—week after week—who develops a ministry relationship with children. Basically, classrooms become places that kids deposit themselves to receive the lesson of the day. Children have no contact with a living, breathing, God-loving adult from church outside of the programmed teaching time.

I believe this practice gives our children a warped view of what it means to take up our cross and follow Christ (Luke 9:23). And what about "Greater love has no one than this, that he lay down his life for his friends" (John 15:13)?

This generation of children needs to see volunteers who are fully committed to the cause of Christ, willing to die for it, and able to go the extra mile. I fear that what many children see in our churches instead is that service to Christ is when it's "convenient to me."

Full rosters of full-time, committed workers is the ideal we all strive for. But what do you do when your reality doesn't match the ideal? You're barely able to recruit part-time workers, much less full-time. If you're in a church or at a place in your volunteer program that you must use part-time volunteers, look for ways to staff your program so children have contact with the same adults consistently in at least one area of your ministry. Try these ideas:

● Have one assisting "relational" teacher who's always in the class but doesn't have to prepare the lesson. The "teaching" teacher rotates with another part-time volunteer to share the teaching load.

● If you have team teachers, when one teacher isn't teaching the lesson, he or she stays in the classroom, focusing on getting to know kids.

● Use part-time teachers for one aspect of your program, such as children's church, and full-time teachers for your Sunday school program.

You may have to try several configurations before you find the right balance for your volunteers and your ministry. But keep working at it until you've established a comfortable level of consistency for the children. Afraid you'll never get enough people to volunteer? Be careful of adjusting your standards to the lowest common denominator. In volunteer recruitment, as with anything in life, you get what you ask for.

"Volunteers who have little expected of them will probably make minimal contribution and soon quit," says Leith Anderson, senior pastor of Wooddale Community Church in Eden Prairie, Minnesota, in the speech, *Stewarding and Motivating Volunteers*. "There is very little satisfaction to doing something below your potential and which doesn't really make much difference. Why bother? By contrast, imagine being asked to do something big and important that will stretch and challenge you...expect a lot from your volunteers and you'll get a lot...expect a little and you'll usually get a little."

● **Keep track of all your volunteer positions.** Since volunteers can join or leave your ministry at any time, coordination is critical. Maintaining an ongoing list of filled and open positions can help you focus your recruiting efforts. "Working in a big church, everyone thinks 'someone else' will do it. Then, no one ends up doing it," says Carmen Kamrath. "At recruiting time, we use a 'countdown' wall, so it's a visual for people to see where we are at filling positions. It also gives a reality boost as to just how many volunteers we need."

The Nursery Schedule is computer software for nursery staffing that can be used effectively for all age groups. It runs on an IBM PC and is available for $199 from HomeFront Software. Call (703) 791-2794.

● **Create job descriptions.** "It takes boldness at the time of enlistment to explain expectations to volunteers," says Darlene Pinson. "We hold our volunteers accountable so we must explain expectations in the beginning."

"Believe me when I say I learned the hard way that being crystal clear regarding job descriptions is essential," says Darlene. "People want (and deserve) to know what will be expected of them. They want to be held accountable. They take pride in doing things well and supporting and accomplishing goals, especially when they have helped set the goals. The vision then becomes important to them."

A job description for each volunteer position is critical for successful recruitment. A detailed job description informs volunteers of what's expected and what they're really getting into. A job description can also serve as an accountability tool—a good measurement for evaluating volunteers to provide positive feedback and helpful suggestions for improvement. Rather than being a binding document, a job description is an effective communication tool.

When developing job descriptions, follow these steps.

● **Get help.** If you've never created job descriptions for your volunteer positions, involve several people in the process. For each job description, invite the current or previous volunteers in that position, an overseer of that position, and a representative from your Christian education board to help you create the job description. You can either meet together formally or have each person give you written input.

Once you've developed the job description, pass it by these people for their detailed edit. Ask them to help you see if you've omitted anything or perhaps required too much.

● **Keep it simple.** Basically, there are five parts to a job description. (See Appendix 1 on page 119 for a sample job description.)

● Job title—Simply, what is this position called?

● Functions—In a few words, what exactly will this person do? What training will be required?

● Accountability—Who will this person answer to? How often will reviews or evaluations be conducted? Will they be formal or informal?

● Term of service—How long will the volunteer serve in this role?

● Acknowledgment—Provide a place at the end of the job description for you and the volunteer to sign. File a signed copy.

In most cases, job descriptions should be no more than a single page. You don't want to overwhelm your volunteers before they've even started! A short, succinct job description will make everyone's job easier.

● **Screen volunteers.** All of them. It's a sad, but true, reality that not everyone who'll volunteer in your program has the children's best interests at heart. "We've developed and implemented a procedure for screening volunteers that incorporates an application and interview as well as a screening form," says Cynthia Petty. It may be one in ten thousand people you'll ever come across who would ever harm a child, but to keep out that one person it's critical to institute careful screening processes.

Richard R. Hammar, Steven W. Klipowicz, and James F. Cobble, Jr., write in their book *Reducing the Risk of Child Sexual Abuse in Your Church,* "A single incident of child molestation can devastate a church and divide the congregation. Members become outraged and bewildered; parents question whether their own children have been victimized; the viability of the church's youth and children's programs is jeopardized; and church leaders face blame and guilt for allowing the incident to happen."

Beyond the corporate implications, any incidence of abuse or molestation can cause a small child to be wounded for the rest of his or her life. God can bring healing, but the fact that such an incident happened in a place that reached out in the name of God makes it even more heinous.

KEEP THEM SAFE

Heather Olson-Bunnell, the minister to children and families at St. Mark's United Methodist Church in Roanoke, Indiana, has developed these guidelines to protect the children in her church.

"1. All adults and youth, employed and volunteer, who work with minors must be screened prior to beginning work.

"2. A Grandparenting rule will be in effect for all adults and youth, employed or volunteer, who have worked with minors in our church prior to the establishment of these guidelines. The master list of such persons will be kept available in the office. These people will not be required to fill out the screening process paperwork.

"3. We will use a 'Two-Person Rule,' that requires employees, volunteers, and supervisors to make every reasonable effort to avoid situations where an employed or volunteer worker is alone with children or youth without a partner.

The two-person rule is mandatory in nursery and kindergarten rooms.

"4. Our 'Open Door Policy' requires the door to a classroom to be open at all times.

"5. All employees and volunteers working with children and youth are required to be members or active constituents of our church for twelve months before they begin to work with minors.

"6. Guidelines for responding to reported incidents of child abuse will be given to all employees and volunteers.

"7. Adults or youth who have been convicted of either sexual or physical abuse of children or youth, or those who have a history of inappropriate conduct with children will not be employed nor allowed to volunteer in any church-sponsored activity or program for minors."

The justice system has no mercy for churches that fail to screen volunteers adequately. And insurance companies are tightening their policies to require churches to have more cautious systems in place for recruiting volunteers. So to be fair to all your volunteers and to provide a safe environment for children, follow all these steps with all your volunteers.

● **Use the six-month rule.** Your initial screening factor should be the amount of time a volunteer has been a member of or has been attending your church. *Never allow anyone who's been in your church for less than six months to serve in children's ministry.* Some churches even require one year.

● **Require applications.** After this time requirement has been fulfilled, have each potential volunteer fill out an application form. See Appendix 2 (p. 120) for a sample application form. (You may also want to add accompanying documents to this application form. For example, Grant Memorial Baptist Church in Winnipeg, Manitoba, requires applicants to sign a statement of faith and an assent to their church's doctrinal statement.) Require all volunteers to complete and sign the form, including the clause releasing personal references from any liability.

● **Conduct interviews.** Once the application is completed, conduct a one-on-one interview with the applicant. Discuss any questions or concerns related to the application form or the job description. Ask them about any previous experiences they've had working with children—good or bad.

● **Check references.** Conduct a thorough reference check of the volunteer. (See Appendix 3 on page 122 for a sample reference check form.) Some children's ministers even recommend getting references from the references, but from a liability standpoint that's unnecessary.

● **Do a criminal background check on every volunteer.** If you do it on only a few, the practice will be offensive. If, on the other hand, you conduct a criminal check on each volunteer for the sake of the children, volunteers will more willingly submit to this practice.

In most areas, you can have a background check run through your local police department for a nominal fee (your church should pay for this!). The applicant must fill out forms and be fingerprinted. Then law enforcement officials will check local and national records. In some communities, volunteers may need to personally request a criminal background check and submit the results to you.

Once all these steps are completed and the volunteer is cleared for joining your team, go over all the paperwork (including the job description) together. Give one copy to the volunteer, and keep a copy in your files.

With positions inventoried, job descriptions created, and volunteer screening policies in place, you're organized and ready to get out into the trenches of volunteer recruitment. As you begin to recruit loving workers to fill your positions, the following section will help you develop a recruiting style that works for you and your ministry.

READY, SET, RECRUIT!

In a discipleship approach to volunteer management, you're not only inviting adults to a significant ministry to children, but you're also bringing them into a life-changing relationship with your team. As you work, you'll no doubt develop your own recruiting style, but if you make these principles the cornerstone of your recruiting, you'll find the job more fulfilling.

● **Pray without ceasing!** The Gospel of Luke tells us that Jesus spent an entire night in prayer before selecting his disciples: "One of those days Jesus went out to a mountainside to pray, and spent the night praying to God. When morning came, he called his disciples to him and chose twelve of them, whom he also designated apostles" (Luke 6:12-13). Can we do anything less?

According to Becky Olmstead, children's pastor at Vineyard Christian Fellowship in Fort Collins, Colorado, prayer and recruiting go hand in hand.

"Recruiting workers for the children's programs in our church is a never-ending job. I've always known that God is the one who provides the workers, but this past year God has challenged me to place a whole new level of dependence on Him.

"In May, I felt that God was leading me to fast, as well as pray, for the workers to staff our summer programs. I, along with my team, fasted and prayed for four days asking God to show us who we were to approach about joining our team. God gave us every single person we needed!

"When it was time to recruit for the fall, prayer with fasting had been so successful that I decided to do it again. After several days of fasting, I felt that God wasn't showing us any people to recruit, and those we did approach weren't interested.

"It became clear that God was trying to get my attention. Using a proven method from the past wasn't what He wanted from me. If I could use past proven recruiting methods, I'd skip building relationship with God and go straight for the results. But God wanted me to come to Him to get my strategy. It is about me being in relationship with Him. God wants me to lead out of my current, vibrant relationship with Him."

"Prayer is always a first step in the recruitment of volunteers," says Clara Olson. "As a recruiter, I am only God's instrument. When we can genuinely accept this reality, recruitment will be an adventure with God. My job becomes one of excitement to connect with the person whom God has selected for leadership."

Tammy Ross has seen tremendous answers to prayer in her ministry to preschoolers at the First Baptist Church in Columbia, Tennessee. "God has done wonderful things in our preschool ministry during the past several years. He has met our needs as they've arisen and he has and is growing our ministry. I've come to realize through prayer that God will not give us the preschoolers and a ministry without the means (teachers, paid staff, facilities, supplies, etc.) by which to carry it out. In his timing, it will all come together!"

● **Recruit without ceasing.** Recruiting is an ongoing process. "My attitude is positively affected when I am realistic and understand that volunteer recruitment is a daily task. It will never be complete!" says Clara Olson. "Why? Because ministry is always changing. Life circumstances are seldom stagnant for long. Few people remain in the same volunteer position in the church more than three years."

So how can you recruit on a daily basis? Keith Johnson who oversees 550 volunteers at Wooddale Community Church says, "Energy is one of my greatest challenges in recruiting because it never lets up! I have to pace myself and my staff. We do a little bit each week rather than waiting 'til August. We have to be creative to figure out where and how to get a hold of people. We try everything—bulletin inserts, adult Sunday school class visits, pulpit announcements, parents, word of mouth, and more."

See "A Week in the Life" (p. 82) for more ongoing, daily recruitment ideas.

● **Recruit in private as well as in public.** Which is better—a personal invitation or a public appeal? I have to admit that I have a bias against public appeals. For church members who aren't involved in children's ministry (as parents or workers), repeated public appeals simply reinforce any weak spots in your current programs and staffing. What comes across is that the children's ministries are always lacking, always in need. Christian education is a negative ministry, so who would want to get involved?

Pastor Harold Bullock of the Hope Baptist Church in Fort Worth, Texas, says there are three inappropriate ways to motivate volunteers. Not surprisingly, at least two of them may involve public appeals. These methods may get people to respond, but they won't get people to stay around for long. Avoid these methods.

The "bind." When people use the bind, they commit people to burdensome things. The bind involves a tactic such as the following. The children's pastor stands up in a service and says, "Everyone who has a child in children's ministry, please stand." Once everyone stands, the children's pastor lowers the boom by saying, "There's no reason that all of you shouldn't volunteer in children's ministry. I want to see all of you at the sign-up table after the service."

The law. It's never appropriate to use the "law" or the Bible to beat up people. Someone may say (in public or private), "Well, the Bible says that parents should train their children, so why aren't you helping in Sunday school?"

Guilt. Be careful about using any kind of guilt to motivate people to get involved. Volunteers solely motivated by guilt are short-termers; they don't have a healthy vision for the ministry or a sense of God's call to the ministry.

An engineer in California was recruited with the guilt method. He says he volunteered because "they had an orientation and they discussed in a lot of detail the problems they were having recruiting people to lead the small groups." When it was time to sign up the next year, this first-grade teacher was gone. He says, "I figured that I had done it for a year and that it was someone else's turn."

If I were queen for the day, I would make this rule: Public appeals for help could only occur after a positive celebration of what God is doing in children's ministry! For example, after a baby parade from the nursery with an upbeat song such as Amy Grant's "Baby, Baby" playing in the background, the children's minister would tell one or two stories about how God has used the nursery to touch young families. Then the plea: "If you'd like to learn how God can use you to share his love with young children and their families, see a member of our nursery team at the children's ministry information table after the service." That's oh-so-different from a litany of needs read from the pulpit!

Chapter 6

"At least once a year a need for volunteers to help with ministry to children is presented from the platform in all our Sunday services," says Clara Olson. "This is done in a variety of ways. People love to see the faces of children. Therefore, a slide presentation can be very effective."

Public appeals may be necessary—and even effective, if handled appropriately—once in a while. But the rest of the time, the best way to recruit is through relationships. "The best recruiting is done one on one," agrees Clara. "Public recruiting may reach people that we hadn't thought about but that God has been convincing. However, it is important to remember that the highest quality volunteer will come through personal contact. For this reason, following a public recruitment presentation, every potential volunteer receives a personal telephone call from the children's pastor or someone on the children's district staff. This is followed by an orientation/training session and in most cases a personal appointment."

● **Get your recruits to recruit others.** People respond to direct appeals from people they know and trust. One survey says that the number one reason people volunteer for a job is because someone asked. Eighty-five percent of adults say they volunteer when they're asked. Ninety-three percent of teenagers volunteer when they're asked (from "Teens Outdo Adults in Volunteering," in the Minneapolis Star Tribune, April 24, 1997; quoted in *Stewarding and Motivating Volunteers* by Leith Anderson).

When you use a shepherding team approach with your volunteers, people will have higher ownership of their ministries and will often be willing to dig in to recruit helpers. "If you measure success by numbers, we have 250 regular volunteers for four Sunday services," says Dwight Mix, children's pastor at Fellowship Bible Church in Lowell, Arkansas, "but we're successful because it's the volunteers who recruit, not just the paid staff."

"The daily task of volunteer recruitment is too big for me to handle alone. It was a great day for me when I realized that present leaders are my best recruiters," says Clara Olson. "Every person already volunteering in children's ministries has a group of people whose lives they touch. Encourage them to share their enthusiasm for their teaching ministry with others. Enthusiasm is contagious!"

Children's pastor Darrell Fraley was once a volunteer in Clara Olson's ministry. Now he says that he's in the business of developing children's pastors. Darrell advocates constant networking as a recruitment strategy. Darrell says there are four stages people pass through in the recruiting phase. These are contacts (names on a list), prospects (names from the list that you've contacted or otherwise followed up on), recruits (people who have agreed to volunteer), and leaders (volunteers who are able to motivate and lead others because they're deeply engaged in their area of service).

"This process is always moving," writes Darrell in his book *Principles of a Purpose-Centered Children's Ministry,* "therefore you always have to be shifting new people into the initial phase of it. This process is also somewhat mathematical. For every ten contacts you'll matriculate a prospect, for every ten prospects you'll matriculate a recruit, for every ten recruits you'll matriculate a leader. And leaders build the ministry."

● **Involve parents in your ministry.** Whether parents like it or not, they're already "involved" in your children's ministry through their children. And while some parents may resist being "recruited" as teachers, you may find other ways for them to get involved. "Many parents seem disconnected from finding their role in children's ministry," says Judy Williamson, a children's minister at St. John's United Methodist Church in Albuquerque, New Mexico. "It's a challenge to help them see the joy in helping children. Some seem to want to get away from their children instead of develop a relationship with their children and their children's friends."

Darrell Fraley has found a way to combat parental malaise and bring on new volunteers. "We doubled our volunteer recruitment on Sunday from sixty last spring to 120 this fall," says Darrell. "This is because of a new paradigm—children's ministry is an extension of the parenting process."

Darrell holds parent/volunteer meetings once a month. He invites them to receive parent training in the context of children's ministry. Darrell also promotes this as a great way for families to stay together at church.

● **Recruit volunteers according to their calling.** Why do you ask people to minister in your children's ministry? Is it because you need things done? Daniel Brown, senior pastor of The Coastlands Church in Aptos, California, and the developer of the Discipleship Video series, How to Get More People to Volunteer, told his congregation, "The whole reason that we invite you to be involved in service is because that's what ministry is and because the only real way for you to discover who and what God made you to be is in the activity of serving other people."

There's been a re-awakening of interest in spiritual gifts in the last two decades, and as church members have discovered their gifts, many have found greater joy in their service. Spiritual gifts—what a great recruiting tool! I just need to locate all the people in my congregation who have the gift of teaching and sign them up. Right? Not necessarily. Using spiritual gifts as your *primary* means to recruit volunteers can cause your recruiting process—and your ministry—to become egocentric rather than God-centered.

God does give us spiritual gifts, and expects us to use them to serve him and serve others. But God also calls us to service—sometimes in areas outside our perceived giftedness. In Exodus 3-4, God called Moses to deliver the Israelites out of slavery. Knowing that this assignment involved convincing, and probably debating with, a hard-hearted opponent, Moses tried to use a "giftless" defense to avoid answering God's call to service. "But I don't have the gift of speaking, Lord," Moses complained. And God responded, "It doesn't matter, because I will be with you."

When God said in Isaiah 6:8, "Whom shall I send? And who will go for us?" Isaiah responded, "Here am I! Send me!" He didn't say, "Me! Me! Me! I have the gift of going!"

Over and over in Scripture, God's call is an obedience issue, not a gift issue. The "called" will either obey or not. Although gifts will be used to complete an assignment from God, God's call is the primary issue.

"Many people today are seeking God's call to ministry or an assignment backwards," write Henry T. Blackaby and Claude V. King in *Experiencing God.* "We teach people to discover their spiritual gifts and then look for an assignment in which they can use their gifts. That can be a frustrating experience for a person looking for their first assignment from God."

"You see a spiritual gift is a manifestation of the Holy Spirit at work through a person in carrying out a God-given assignment," Blackaby and King continue. "Normally, a person will not know their spiritual giftedness without first receiving an assignment. When God gives an assignment, a person obeys and God accomplishes what He intended through the person. The evidence of God's supernatural activity is what we usually identify as spiritual gifts. A person who has never accepted an assignment will not likely know or see his or her spiritual gifts."

Sandy Gauby, a teachers aide and mother of two, says she first got involved in children's ministry at Fellowship Bible Church in Lowell, Arkansas, because of God's call on her life. "I initially got involved in children's ministry because I felt like that was the Lord's calling for me at that time," Sandy says. "I volunteer in my church's children's ministry because I feel like it's a way to give back to the Lord—that if he gives you a certain gift that you need to use it. I don't know if my gift is necessarily teaching, but it is to work with children."

Ask people to seek God's will as they consider serving in children's ministry. What are each person's passions? What burdens do they already carry? Gifts are only part of the ministry mix that makes up an effective volunteer. It's critical to encourage volunteers to minister out of a calling from God—because when God calls someone to a task, he'll enable that person to complete it!

As you ask people to determine God's call on their life, call out what you see in them that makes you think God might be shaping them to be part of your team. Remember to call people to the vision, not just the position. As you share your vision with people, ask them to pray about whether God would have them become a part of fulfilling the vision. When we stop short of connecting people to the vision, we make it harder for them to discern whether God is truly calling them to serve.

My husband Mike and I have been taking a parenting class at our church. One day, I jumped up to get a tissue and was met halfway by one of the leaders. "Would you and your husband like to teach this class next time?" My response was incredulity. "What? Oh my! But we have so much to learn!" He said, "Well why don't you think about it?"

Mike and I went home and thought about it, but we weren't quite sure what we were supposed to be thinking about. We kept asking each other why he would've asked us. Was it something he saw in us that distinguished us from the other parents? Or, was he under a deadline to recruit new leaders and I was just the first one to jump up with a sneeze? We weren't sure if we should be affirmed or not.

When you tell someone that you believe that God has a place for them in children's ministry, point out why. Lon Flippo, a children's ministry consultant for the Assemblies of God, says to "always call out something in the person that you're recruiting, such as what you've seen in them. Say 'You're so good with kids; you'd be great in our children's ministry' or 'You're hilarious! Kids would love you.' This is especially effective with men; they're putty in your hands."

If we fail to encourage our volunteers to seek God's calling in their lives, we pay the price later when volunteers end up questioning God's will. For example, Laurie Labrato from Cantonment, Florida, recently resigned from children's ministry after five years of service.

"I quit primarily because my husband and I had served in that position for five years," she says. "I have always worked with children. I've always been led to work with children, but my husband chose that primarily because that's where I've always served. And we wanted to serve together. And I feel that in the last couple of years he's really been searching if that's exactly the role the Lord had for both of us. And we're really praying because, who knows, the Lord may lead us back into the children's ministry."

"I really feel like you do need to search your heart and stand back and listen to God," Laurie says. "I think so many times we do things just because we've always done them that way. In the case here, we're sitting quietly and listening for a change. Lord is this where you want us to be?

So many times we volunteer for things without seeking his will and that's of utmost importance."

Dana Janney, third- and fourth-grade supervisor at Whittier Hills Baptist Church in LaHabra, California, says, "We're reducing turnover by finding out what people's heartbeat for ministry is, and then finding ways to help them grow in that area. We try to find the right 'fit' for the given need within the ministry."

So, rather than recruiting people according to their spiritual gifting, we need to recruit people according to their spiritual calling. At my church, The Church of the Good Shepherd in Loveland, Colorado, our church leaders were very clear that they didn't want anyone to volunteer to help in any role in our move to two services if they didn't feel called by God. They told us not to come out of a sense of guilt, but rather to seek God and ask him to tell us what he was calling us to. Now every position is filled.

WHEN ALL ELSE FAILS

If after you've done everything, you still don't have enough volunteers, what'll you do?

The typical reaction to such a scenario has been to keep the program going and beg more people to volunteer. The problem with this approach, which I've mentioned earlier, is that it facilitates a dysfunctional situation where you become the person who'll prop up the unhealthy program.

Instead of plunging headlong into a massive recruiting blitz to save a dying program, put it out of its misery. If you truly believe that God won't call you to a ministry without providing everything you need, you'll want to carefully scrutinize any ministry that constantly lacks volunteers.

"The greatest challenge in recruiting volunteers is waiting on God. Sometimes God doesn't build his team as quickly as I have calendared," says Judy Basye, children's pastor at First Baptist of San Mateo, California. David wanted to build the temple for God, but the timing wasn't right until Solomon came along. Perhaps God is calling you to a ministry but the timing isn't right.

Or consider that God may be pruning your ministry

for greater fruit in the future. If you resist, you may miss out on something better. So as hard as it may be, cancel a program that isn't fully staffed. Do less with more. Do those things that God has provided for. If people struggle with your decision, invite them to pray with you until the right people step forward to fully staff the program.

Clara Olson understands this principle. For Clara, there's no frantic search to fill slots. If she doesn't have enough volunteers to staff a program, the program doesn't exist. The truth is: Clara does things backward. She waits on God before she leaps, sometimes waiting as long as two years for God to raise up the leadership for a ministry she's dreamed about.

So "trust the Lord with all your heart and lean not on your own understanding" (Proverbs 3:5). In all your recruitment efforts, in all your programs, in your whole ministry, acknowledge him, and he will clear the way for you to go forward with your ministry.

Stop & Consider	Read the book of Nehemiah. List all the ways you see God's role in getting the work done. Then list ways Nehemiah depended on God. How can you depend on God in your recruitment and other ministry efforts?

A WEEK IN THE LIFE

What's life like for Sondra Saunders, senior preschool and children's minister at Prestonwood Baptist in Dallas, Texas, as she manages her volunteer ministry? Take a peek into her recruiting diary. First of all, everything begins with prayer.

"It's the first day of January and Lord, as I think of all that is ahead of me with the many, many ministries to enlist and train for, I ask for your guidance and wisdom. You know the needs, Lord, better than I do. Please guide me to the right people who love children and those who will be willing to teach them about you.

"**Sunday afternoon**—Call the couple who indicated in the New Members class this morning that they were interested in teaching kindergarten. Ask them to observe next Sunday morning in a department, and then meet with them Wednesday evening to go over the job descriptions, responsibilities, etc.

"Write an appreciation note to the first-grade director who did such a beautiful job with the Bible story this a.m.

"Monday morning—Write an appreciation note to the new greeters at children's booth yesterday—thank them for the way they made new families feel welcome.

"Call parents of our second-grade department who aren't presently serving elsewhere and let them know of the two vacancies of teachers in their child's room. If they will not commit to teaching regularly, see if they will substitute (this will let them know firsthand of the immediate needs).

"Write an appreciation note to the couple who observed last Sunday in the two-year-old department. Set up an appointment as soon as possible to discuss with them further opportunities for service.

"Monday afternoon—Secure a list of stay-at-home parents to begin calling vacation Bible school leaders. Also, pull the VBS file from last year and call those leaders.

"Tuesday—Ask adult minister to…provide names of possible leaders for Sunday school.

"Contact parents who might help sponsor our pre-teen retreat. Set up a meeting with these parents.

"Wednesday morning—Call parents who have indicated that they want more information on Bible drill. Set up a meeting to explain curriculum and procedures.

"Wednesday afternoon—Greet parents as they drop off their children for Awana. Talk to as many parents as possible to let them know how special their children are and how much Scripture they are learning. Tell the parents that if they are not serving anywhere in the church, we have great needs for leadership.

"Thursday morning—Call any Awana parents who expressed interest in serving. Set up appointments to explain responsibilities and expectations.

"Thursday afternoon—Call Amy Burns; she indicated two months ago (according to my file) that she would be willing to teach in February. Get her to attend a training session for four-year-olds in two weeks. Send her a written notice also.

"Write an appreciation letter to all the faithful nursery directors. Let them know I'll be praying for each one of them this year.

"Friday morning—Call the new families of preschoolers who have joined our church this past month. Ask them to assist in our volunteer program once a month.

"Friday afternoon—Enlist additional people to serve as greeters on Sunday morning at our three greeter booths. We need twelve people per

Sunday and are short by three on most Sundays.

"Saturday morning—Call Linda Dodge and Jennifer Byrd. They both indicated (according to notes in my file) that they would consider a place of service following the holidays. I need to follow up on them today!"

A great resource to help volunteers discover their passions, spiritual gifts, and ministry styles is *Network.* Available from Willow Creek Resources for $44.98. Call 800-570-9812.

Chapter 7

TRAINING MODELS

Jesus left there and went to his hometown, accompanied by his disciples. When the Sabbath came, he began to teach in the synagogue, and many who heard him were amazed.

"Where does this man get these things?" they asked. "What's this wisdom that has been given him, that he even does miracles! Isn't this the carpenter? Isn't this Mary's son and the brother of James, Joseph, Judas and Simon? Aren't his sisters here with us?" And they took offense at him.

Jesus said to them, "Only in his hometown, among his relatives and in his own house is a prophet without honor."

—Mark 6:1-4

Training volunteers can be a tricky business. Just as the people in Jesus' home town resisted his teaching, some volunteers naturally take offense at the idea that they need to be "trained." They wouldn't have volunteered, they reason, if they didn't have gifts or skills in their area of service. Or maybe they've been working in children's ministry for years and think they know all the tricks. Training, they insist, is for new volunteers who are "learning the ropes."

Yet Scripture is clear on the importance of teaching—even for seasoned volunteers. Proverbs 9:9 says, "Instruct a wise man and he will be wiser still; teach a righteous man and he will add to his learning." Jesus himself never stopped teaching. Just before it records the events leading up to Jesus' death, the Gospel of Luke says: "Each day Jesus was teaching at the temple, and each evening he went out to spend the night on the hill called the Mount of Olives, and all the people came early in the morning to hear him at the temple" (Luke 21:37-38). Even Jesus' last meal with his inner circle is punctuated with teaching—about his example of servanthood, his love for the Father, and his eventual return (John 13:1-17; 14:15-26; 16:16-33).

Even though some people may resist at first, it's critical to give volunteers the training they need to be successful in the classroom—for the sake of the children. "The learning environment today looks very different from what volunteers grew up in," says Todd Crouch, Sabbath school director at Worldwide Church of God in Scenery Hill, Pennsylvania. "If we're not careful, volunteers will continue to do the same old things simply because that's all they know. We need to capitalize on opportunities to train volunteers in new ways to reach today's children."

Training can also increase volunteer longevity by enabling volunteers to successfully manage potentially frustrating situations they encounter in the classroom. Debbie Weisen, children's minister at Spokane Valley Nazarene Church in Spokane, Washington, says "With so many troubled kids in our program, teaching can become nothing more than an hour of discipline. That's not fun or rewarding."

In a nutshell, fully trained volunteers will have the most rewarding ministry experience. According to Leith Anderson, "The best organizations not only offer high expectations but also strong enabling. When I agree to challenges beyond my experience and you help me to achieve those challenges, I feel very good about you and very good about myself. That motivates me to volunteer again and try something more challenging. If you keep raising the standard and keep helping me reach that standard, we have a synergy that makes us all winners."

In western education, training encompasses two different but equally important models: classroom training and apprenticeship training. In classroom training, the teacher exposes students to ideas. The students then transfer those ideas to their work. In apprenticeship training, the teacher models skills and develops in the individual the ability to do well. Rather than use one model to the exclusion of the other, use both. In the team, training is more personalized and specific to people's needs. In large group or classroom training, volunteers sense that they're part of something bigger than their team. Momentum and excitement are enhanced.

Before you strike your balance between classroom and apprenticeship training, you'll need to determine what it is that your volunteers need to know. With your team, set your training standards in these three areas:

1. What does each volunteer need to know?
2. What does each volunteer need to do?
3. What does each volunteer need to be?

For example, your standards may look something like this:

Each volunteer needs to
- recite our children's ministry mission statement,
- read our church's doctrinal statement,
- know what to do with out-of-the-norm kids,

- understand how to help children with attention deficit hyperactivity disorder (ADHD),
- know how to lead a child to Christ,
- understand the lesson book,
- understand why kids do what they do,
- be aware of age-level characteristics,
- know classroom management skills, and
- know how to pray.

Each volunteer needs to
- have faith in Christ as his or her savior,
- spend time in God's Word regularly,
- have a consistent prayer life,
- value children,
- articulate their faith, and
- respond to teachable moments.

Each volunteer needs to
- have exemplary classroom ethics,
- grow in Christian character,
- be filled with the fruit of the Spirit, and
- be committed to God's purposes of bringing people into the family of God and teaching them to grow.

Once you've determined what your training standards are—or what you want volunteers to become—determine which of these standards are best taught in an apprentice relationship and which in a classroom situation. For example, the best way to teach someone to respond to teachable moments is for them to see someone responding to teachable moments in a classroom. However, volunteers could first be taught about ADHD in a classroom setting and then gain additional expertise by watching a master teacher deal with children with ADHD.

It's not always a black-and-white issue, but it often works well to teach a concept in a large group and then reinforce it in an apprenticeship situation. "It's a challenge for me to find the time to do an in-depth training time," says Selma Johnson, minister to children/family life at Northway Baptist Church in Dallas, Texas. Selma has overcome this problem with a creative and practical solution. "We put an experienced teacher and an inexperienced teacher together," she says. "I've found that the inexperienced teacher will learn more and be more excited about learning more."

Read on to discover how you can make apprenticeships a regular part of your volunteer training program.

Apprenticeship has been called many things. Today, "mentoring" is the buzzword for apprenticeship. In essence, it's a life-on-life proposition; one person learns from another person's life. And it's the same sort of relationship Jesus entered into with his followers. In Luke 6:40, Jesus says that "a student is not above his teacher, but everyone who is fully trained will be like his teacher."

As ministry workers, our goal for ourselves—and the people we mentor—is to be like our teacher, Jesus. Daniel Brown even suggests that the fundamental curriculum for a discipleship ministry is found in Matthew 28:19-20: "Therefore go and make disciples of all nations...teaching them to obey everything I have commanded you." Brown goes on to say, "A discipler teaches others whatever it is that Jesus has taught you."

Jesus was the master teacher. He was God's Son, and he knew everything. But his disciples were ordinary people like you and me. They certainly didn't know everything Jesus knew, but their lack of knowledge didn't stop Jesus from sending them out to disciple others, nor did it stop them from carrying out Jesus' commission. So if you or anyone involved in your ministry is worried they don't know enough to disciple others, relax. A trainer or discipler doesn't have to know everything! In fact, "I don't know enough" is never a good excuse for people not to be in a discipleship relationship with others.

Successful apprenticeships can be powerful, even life-changing experiences. Keith Johnson, pastor to children at Wooddale Church in Eden Prairie, Minnesota, remembers the successful apprenticeship of one volunteer in his ministry:

"Matt was an outstanding artist. He worked with the animators of *The Simpsons* and *Toy Story*. When Matt came to work for children's ministry he brought a freshness that was very exciting for children and their classrooms. Matt, however, didn't relate well with adults. When we hire volunteers, however, we get them because of their strengths and not their weaknesses.

"We countered Matt's weaknesses with good greeters at the doors of classrooms and very appropriate letters home to parents that gave them information they needed to calm their innate concerns of what their child would be learning. Matt wasn't frustrated because we didn't expect him to improve in that area. But improve he did. When the expectation for him to produce great activities and sets for kids was allowed to run free, he became a learner by watching other adults handle parents. He was taught by the fact that the team had balance and respect for each other's differences."

TEAM-BASED APPRENTICESHIPS

If your volunteers are already organized into teams (see Chapter 4 for more information on how to do this), it's just a short step to incorporate team-based training through the apprenticeship model. "Having people come to training in a group is a challenge. They want individualized instruction only at a time convenient to them," says Judy Williamson, children's minister at St. John's United Methodist Church in Albuquerque, New Mexico. "That's why team-based training is so effective."

"We have team leaders who oversee certain departments for one of our two services," says Debbie Neufeld, the children's minister at Grant Memorial Baptist Church in Winnipeg, Manitoba. "These team leaders care for their teams of people who serve within their departments. As the years go by, we are seeing more and more of these leaders being interested in the lives of their workers—encouraging them, supporting them, getting involved in their lives. I feel this is strengthening our ministry as we minister to one another and bond together as we serve in children's ministry."

FIVE-STEP TRAINING

1. Tell why scripturally.
2. Show them how.
3. Get them started.
4. Keep them going.
5. Get them to train others.

Dwight Mix also involves his team leaders in the training process. "We are currently adding to what we do," says Dwight, the children's pastor at Fellowship Bible Church in Lowell, Arkansas. "We 'kick off' the year with a dinner and group activities night in August. These activities help build 'team spirit' among the different volunteer groups. We're adding some great ideas from Ty Rose's training materials from Saddleback Community Church. These are given to the volunteers in 'nuggets' on Sunday mornings."

Debbie Gibson, one of Dwight's volunteers, says, "In our church's new program called 'Snip It/Clip It,' our team leader takes us out once a month and does a little five-minute program. This time we had one on discipline. She just takes a few of us each Sunday."

"Snip It/Clip It" is working for Dwight's church. But each team leader will configure his or her team differently. Perhaps in your church one team leader will provide training for each team member. In another ministry, a team leader may decide to match newer teachers with master teachers in a training relationship. At a minimum, you should require your team leaders to do the following with their teams on a monthly basis: pray for, train, encourage, befriend, and hold team members accountable. Use the Appendix 5: "Team Leader Report" (p. 124) to meet with your team leaders monthly to ensure that this training is ongoing and teams are functioning well.

For leaders who are working individually with team members in a discipling relationship, see the "Individual Training Chart" (p. 125). (A blank chart has been provided for you in Appendix 6 on page 125.) In a training

INDIVIDUAL TRAINING CHART

Name	Goal	Present Situation	Forces Helping	Forces Hindering	Steps to Goal
Tammy Smith	To improve her outreach to children.	Guests are sporadic, but she wants to bring in more children.	*Loves kids. *Children are eager to invite their friends.	*Works full time so she's busy. *Doesn't know any children apart from church.	*Encourage her to work with her team teacher to plan a party for kids to invite friends to. *Brainstorm how to mobilize kids in outreach to their friends. *Have her talk to a teacher who excels at outreach.
	To develop patience within the classroom.	Irritable with children when they make messes.	*Loves kids. *Recognizes the problem.	*Short temper. *Desire to control the classroom tightly.	*Go over age-level character-istics so she'll understand what kids can be expected to do. *Co-teach a class to model for her. *Help her recon-sider her class-room goals to allow for less control and more discovery.

situation, have the team leader determine the volunteer's goal(s). Then have the team leader note the volunteer's present situation. What are the forces helping the person achieve the goal? What are the forces hindering the volunteer from succeeding? Then have the team leader determine what steps will be taken to help the volunteer reach the goal.

CLASSROOM TRAINING

Individual team-based apprenticeship training is balanced by additional classroom or large group training sessions. As we discussed at the beginning of this chapter, getting volunteers to attend training sessions isn't easy. In fact, all children's ministry volunteer managers agree that getting volunteers to attend training sessions is perhaps the most difficult part of their job. So how do you get volunteers to come?

The first step to increase attendance at training meetings is to require volunteers to attend. If it's optional, you'll get only the cream of the crop. If you require training in volunteers' job descriptions and they agree to the requirements up front, you can hold volunteers accountable to attend training.

Last spring, I led a teacher training meeting on a Saturday morning at our church; 25 percent of the volunteers came. This year with Teacher Enrichment, I knew I didn't want to repeat that again—all that work, so little return. Then one of our children's church leaders came up with an ingenious idea. Our church's Sunday morning children's ministry time encompasses Sunday school and children's church during the adult worship time. Once a month, during children's church time, the kids have "Video Sunday." Why not train the teachers during this time? Teachers are there already; they aren't needed in children's church; they have no place to go; and no excuses! It seemed like a guaranteed way to get 100 percent involvement.

So far, we've had about 80 percent of our teachers attend. I think part of our problem is that we never made attendance a requirement in the recruiting phase. The meetings seem to be helpful to those who attend; volunteers have said things like, "Everyone needs to come to this!"

At first, I was discouraged by the numbers. Where were the other 20 percent? Then God changed my perspective and reminded me to celebrate that we had tripled our attendance ratio! We had three times as many teachers coming!

I'm not sure that it's possible to get 100 percent attendance at training meetings. (If you're getting that, please call me; I want to hear from you.) Bonnie Newell, children's pastor at Breiel Boulevard Church of God in Middletown, Ohio, says, "I personally have a philosophy that I train those who come. And the others? I can't change their lack of desire for training."

Of all the children's ministers and volunteers I talked to, no one said that training was struggle-free. But each person had come up with creative solutions to the training challenge that may actually help you double—or even triple—your efforts. I hope so.

Time is a premium commodity for volunteers, so any meetings you schedule must have these "worth-my-time principles." Use these principles to help volunteers realize that they're spending their time wisely by coming to a large group training.

● **Flexibility.** Offer the same training several times in case volunteers have a schedule conflict. Clara Olson, Family Life Pastor at New Hope Community Church in Portland, Oregon, says that at her church "ministry training for volunteers is offered three times each week: Wednesdays 9:30 a.m. or 5:30 p.m. and Sundays 5:00-6:15 p.m."

Or provide flexibility by offering different training packages that may better fit into volunteers' busy schedules. Covering the same information each time allows volunteers to attend at least one session and get the training you want them to have.

"We use a variety of options: an all-day Saturday, a series of Wednesday nights, and a series of Sunday mornings during Sunday school," says Steven Wood, minister of Christian education at Westwood Church in Evansville, Indiana. "We also have a six-hour workshop that we've developed."

● **Convenience.** It's difficult to get volunteers to come back to church for training sessions. So why not schedule training when volunteers are already at the church?

"We schedule training times during services when everyone is on site," says Paul Duris, children's pastor at East Hill Foursquare Church in Gresham, Oregon. "It's more work for me, but it's worth the effort in terms of percentage of turnout."

"We're a regional church," says Dwight Mix, "so getting workers to come back to 'an event' to train them is especially difficult. So we do training when our volunteers are here at church—namely on Sunday mornings or right after church, and we provide lunch."

Cynthia Petty, the director of grade school ministry at Lake Pointe Baptist Church in Rockwall, Texas. also trains on Sunday mornings. "We have monthly orientation meetings that provide training to our new leaders," she says. "They miss a worship service but receive a tape of the message. We also have quarterly training meetings that provide training for the upcoming quarter as well as fun and fellowship."

Sondra Saunders, senior preschool and children's minister at Prestonwood Baptist in Dallas, Texas, says she "offers training at the most convenient time—Sunday afternoons—and provides a snack supper."

● **Creativity.** Call your training time something creative. How about "Recharge" or "TNL" (The Next Level)? There's something about the word "training" anymore that people just don't like. Give your training a fun and creative name.

And be creative in planning the components of your time. Keith Johnson offers creative training. When volunteers come to training, they meet with their teams and then have four choices of twenty-minute workshops on topics such as discipline and storytelling.

Vary your format and add creative elements each time. Ty Rose's staff at Saddleback Community Church in Mission Viejo, California, took a potentially snoozer topic and made it hilariously creative. For a meeting on fire safety, they got fire hats from a carnival supply company. When teachers entered the room, they got hats with their lunches and candy "fire" sticks in them. Large-screen televisions showed scenes from *Backdraft* while songs such as "We Didn't Start the Fire" and "Fire and Rain" played in the background. For door prizes, they gave fire extinguishers, garden hoses, and smoke alarms. For part of the training, they presented a funny skit on what not to do in the classroom when there's a fire.

Meet with your team and use this checklist to brainstorm about creative elements for your next training meeting:

● What props apply to our theme?
● How could we decorate our room to creatively convey our topic?
● Are there any fun food tie-ins?
● What creative theme-related items could we give away?
● Are there any movies or songs that fit our theme?
● How could we convey our theme in drama, music, or art?
● What element of humor can we add to our meeting?

● **Comfort.** Keep it casual and comfortable. Always provide child care, and make sure kids have good snacks.

● **Relevance.** Start with the standards you've established for your training program. But in addition to these, ask volunteers what they want to cover in training times. Distribute index cards periodically and have volunteers list their number one need in their ministry right now. Observe volunteers and listen to recurring issues so you can best pinpoint the topics that'll meet their current needs.

● **Timeliness.** Keep it convenient and succinct. Start on time and end on time. There's nothing more irritating to a punctual, busy person than leaders who don't honor their unwritten contract of start and end times.

Start every meeting when the first person walks in. Have theme-related activities planned to engage volunteers right away. For example, you might have volunteers form pairs, have one partner tie up the other with yarn, then give the tied-up volunteer one minute to try to get free.

• **Regularity.** How often you meet with volunteers is up to you, but whatever schedule you choose, stick to it! Some children's ministry workers meet weekly, others meet monthly or quarterly. Here are some sample schedule ideas to get you started.

• Carmen Kamrath has training at the beginning of the year for everyone; quarterly topical growth/training; and optional weekly leadership training.

• Dann Lies has monthly meetings with teachers and biannual meetings with everyone else.

• Mary Eagle provides two workshops a year, one retreat a year, and ongoing training as needed.

• Debbie Neufeld provides monthly "huddle" times and quarterly vision times. Children's ministry adults also have video-training for leadership meetings and monthly skill development sessions. Debbie says, "The various departments meet together to problem-solve, touch base and mutually encourage one another. We have monthly lunches after church for our preschool department to meet; our grades 1-6 leaders meet during our break time between the services. Our team leaders lead the huddle times with their own team."

• Keith Johnson leads a parent/teacher partnership series and a new volunteer orientation in addition to other training opportunities.

Get input from your volunteers, then schedule regular trainings at optimal times. The possibilities are as varied as the people in your ministry!

• **Relational.** Remember that volunteers want to connect with one another. Get volunteers talking to and interacting with one another as they discover the truths you want them to learn. For example, our last teacher enrichment meeting looked like this:

I wanted volunteers to learn how to make kids feel special and valued. So before volunteers arrived, I decorated the room door and set out breakfast parfaits on a decorated table. I greeted each volunteer warmly and directed them to the snack table. The volunteers then gathered with other teachers in their age-group team.

Different people gave celebration reports of the good things God had done in and through them in their ministries this month. I then gave away door prizes—resources they could use in their ministry. I gathered them together for a group photo, and asked them, "What has anyone in this room done today to make you feel special?" After their answers, I had them brainstorm in their teams how to make kids in their age group feel special. We then listed their answers one by one on newsprint. Then we gathered in a circle and closed in a prayer of celebration for them.

I repeated the same process in the next Teacher Enrichment meeting that morning, except I wouldn't allow these volunteers to repeat any of the ideas that were already listed. Our volunteers came up with eighteen great ideas to make kids feel special. I typed up their answers and mailed them to all the teachers—even those who didn't attend.

Maybe I could've come up with twenty-five great ways to make kids feel special. I could've droned on and on about how to do this, but it would've been only a fraction as effective as the process of volunteers "discovering" these things together.

● **Nourishing.** Always provide good food! For every teacher-enrichment meeting, I provide the best breakfast food possible. We've had Danish and coffee, breakfast parfaits, and this week we're having flavored coffees, biscotti, and scones. (I've even toyed with having a coffee shop bring in their espresso machine, but I'm afraid I'll blow our budget.) The food you serve communicates value to your volunteers. Give them food fit for kings and queens!

Hopefully, incorporating these ideas will boost your attendance as you develop training experiences that your volunteers will enjoy. However, even if attendance isn't 100 percent, you'll be able to rest assured that you've gone the extra mile to provide excellent training for those who are willing to be trained.

ALTERNATIVE TRAINING IDEAS

What about those volunteers who just can't seem to get to training, no matter when you schedule it? Remember, training doesn't always have to happen in a regular classroom setting. Try these new ideas for training your volunteers when it's most convenient for them.

● **Portable Orientation.** "It's so difficult to pull volunteers out of busy schedules to attend training," says Kevin Reimer, pastor to children and families at Lake Avenue Church in Pasadena, California. "So we developed 'The Portable Orientation' audiocassette along with a link training manual, designed to be listened to during the morning L.A. commute."

● **Seminars.** Send one or two volunteers to the same seminar. Then have them return and share with other volunteers what they've learned. "We send all volunteers to our local Christian Workers Conference in March every year," says Debbie Wiesen.

- **Newsletters.** "It's a challenge to work around volunteers' busy schedules," says Mary Eagle, director of religious education for children at St. Cecilia in Beaverton, Oregon. "We make as few demands on their time as possible. Instead of meetings, we hand out a weekly letter and newsletter to be read when they have time."

- **Book club.** Assign a Christian education book for your volunteers to read. Then bring them together to discuss the book.

- **Lunch bunch.** Meet with volunteers for lunch and a brief training time. Plan several brown bag lunches a month in different places. Provide the same training each time to make lunch training convenient for all of your volunteers.

- **Shadows.** Have a volunteer shadow you throughout an entire day. At the end of the day, ask your shadow what he or she learned.

- **Resources.** Make available books, tapes, videos, and magazines. Debbie Neufeld's team members pass around a Treat 'n' Training bag with resources and goodies.

- **Living lessons.** Lead by personal example, or have another person share how he or she has learned about a topic.

As you develop a well-rounded training program, above all, be creative! Keep working at it until you develop the mix of team-based apprenticeship training, classroom training, and alternative training ideas that works for your ministry.

| **Stop & Consider** | Read Psalm 25:4-5; Psalm 86:11-12; Psalm 119:33-37. What has the Lord been teaching you lately? How will you teach these things to your volunteers? |

TRAINING PROGRAM

Clara Olson, Family Life Pastor at New Hope Community Church in Portland, Oregon, describes her training program.

"A typical children's ministries training hour begins with refreshments and fellowship while people are arriving. This time is so important in team development because of the relational aspect. Fun songs followed by more worshipful songs and prayer fill the next segment of time. After prayer comes announcements or organizational information. Sometimes we use this time for ministry and praise reports. Our time together is concluded with twenty-five minutes of teaching.

"We have discovered that people are most comfortable at training when seated at round tables. This kind of seating arrangement offers a natural flow for prayer circles and discussion groups.

"Prayer time is very important! Sometimes I pray for the group as a whole. But more often they pray for each other's needs in their small groups. Occasionally, anyone with a special need is invited to sit in a chair in the center of the room so that everyone can gather around, lay hands on and pray. We have experienced amazing answers to prayer by following this Scriptural plan.

"Teaching topics are broad in scope because we want them to be appropriate to any children's worker. In each training session there will be people representing Sunday school, children's church, Kids Clubs, Positive Action Support Groups, Music Ministry, nursery, and others. Some topics are: 'Leading a Child to Christ,' 'Classroom Management Skills,' 'Age-Group Characteristics,' or 'Helping Children Through Crises.' We also try to use a variety of teaching methods in order to be good models for our leaders. Volunteers also need encouragement in personal growth. Therefore, some teaching is designed for that purpose. Where more specific training is required as with Neighborhood Kids Clubs, we have a once a month extended training time.

"The need for love, acceptance, relationships, encouragement, inspiration, motivation, and laughter is a powerful force in all our lives. When ministry training speaks to these needs, we can be sure that our volunteers will want to be consistent in attendance at training. When they are consistent in training, they will be consistently successful in ministry."

Chapter 8

WAY TO GO! GOOD JOB!

As soon as Jesus was baptized, he went up out of the water. At that moment heaven was opened, and he saw the Spirit of God descending like a dove and lighting on him.

And a voice from heaven said, "This is my Son, whom I love; with him I am well pleased."

—Matthew 3:16-17

This is what affirmation is all about in your children's ministry. As you show your appreciation for your volunteers, it's as though they're hearing God say, "This is my child whom I love—with whom I am well pleased!"

Showing appreciation to your volunteers gives them a sense of satisfaction and increases their desire to stay with your ministry long-term. Leith Anderson, senior pastor at Wooddale Church in Eden Prairie, Minnesota, says, "Volunteers must be paid just like employees. The difference is that they are not paid with money. They are paid with less tangible but very important rewards. Volunteers must sense that they are getting as much or more out of their volunteering than they are putting into it. Otherwise they will quit."

Dwight Mix, children's pastor at Fellowship Bible Church in Lowell, Arkansas, agrees. He says, "This past year we were able to 'keep' or have most of our volunteers come back. That was due to a large part to the numerous times we did things to appreciate our volunteers."

Dwight's children's ministry staff coordinates a Sunday morning brunch for each of their four services. After volunteers have served in a service, the volunteers are served brunch with the ministry staff and kids. "Every worker expresses to us that this alone makes them feel appreciated!" says Dwight. "We also do a small gift about four times a year."

Carmen Kamrath, the children's ministries director at Community Church of Joy in Glendale, Arizona, manages over two hundred volunteers who minister to over one thousand children. Affirmation can be a daunting task with this many volunteers. Carmen says, "With so many volunteers, it's tough to make sure they feel appreciated and part of the team."

Carmen works hard to affirm her volunteers. A few tools in her goody basket: encouragement notes and goodies, monthly phone calls, and special dinners, lunches, or breakfasts. Carmen has also enlisted "coaches" to keep weekly contact with volunteers.

In this chapter, you'll find tons of affirmation ideas to help you show your undying appreciation for your volunteers. But before we dive into the ideas, let's look at what Jesus praised and where genuine appreciation comes from.

Jesus' Affirmations

Although I want to give you hundreds of ideas to help you show appreciation to your volunteers, I don't want you to think that genuine appreciation is a "program." Quite the opposite! Genuine appreciation flows from a genuinely appreciative heart. It comes from a heart filled with sincere love for others.

It's obvious to people when you really care for them. Think about how you feel when you love someone—either an adult or a child. Your heart softens, your eyes change—you emit love particles to that person! If you don't have genuine love, all of these ideas will be delivered as cold projects rather than "warm fuzzies."

I remember a time that I felt genuine love from a volunteer coordinator. One Sunday morning I stopped to sign in my four-year-old daughter Abby at her preschool class. Kari Stewart was on the floor with the children, interacting with them. When she turned and saw me, her face lit up and she brightly said, "Hi, Chris!" My heart actually leapt a little that this person was so excited to see me. Believe me, when Kari asked me to help with the preschool program at vacation Bible school that summer, I had no problem saying yes. I feel genuinely cared for by Kari.

Genuine appreciation is also strongest when it speaks to the heart. To speak to volunteers' hearts, affirm what Jesus affirmed in people. Look for instances when your volunteers display one of the characteristics that Jesus praised, such as the following.

● **Faith.** It seemed as though Jesus was often taken aback by instances of faith in a faithless generation. He was quick to praise people when they demonstrated even the tiniest expression of faith. Jesus praised the Roman centurion who said, "Just say the word and my servant will be healed"

(Matthew 8:9). He also praised the faith of the woman with an issue of blood who touched his garment (Luke 8:48); the woman who kept asking him to heal her demon-possessed daughter (Matthew 15:28); and the friends who brought a paralytic on a bed through the ceiling (Matthew 9:2).

● **Gratitude.** A person who knows he or she has been forgiven much loves much. Jesus praised the woman who washed his feet with her tears (Luke 7:47) and the one cleansed Samaritan leper who returned to thank him as nine others ran away (Luke 17:16-19).

● **Humility.** Jesus honored those who seemed to seek honor the least. Jesus said that whoever humbles himself as a child is greatest in God's kingdom (Matthew 18:4). According to Jesus, we're blessed if we're aware of our spiritual poverty (Matthew 5:3); and we're blessed if we bear insults for Christ's name (Luke 6:22-23).

● **Generosity.** Jesus appreciated people who had an eternal economy that resulted in earthly generosity. Jesus praised the widow who tithed two mites and gave all she had out of her poverty (Luke 21:2-4); Jesus praised those who gave food to the hungry, drink to the thirsty, hospitality to strangers, clothes to the naked, and companionship to the sick and imprisoned (Matthew 25:34-36).

In all these examples, Jesus looked beyond the externals to the heart. He was always quick to praise the good that he saw in people. Therefore, we can follow his example with our volunteers. Use ideas in this chapter to help you point out the good that you see in the people who serve in your ministry.

Appreciation Events

Judy Williamson, director of children's ministries at St. John's United Methodist Church in Albuquerque, New Mexico, says that to affirm volunteers she hosts an "All Educators Event." "Our education ministries work area holds a dinner for all Sunday school teachers, registrars, data input volunteer staff, substitutes, preschool teachers, Scout leaders, music teachers, art teachers, and Advent festival leaders to meet one another and affirm one another's ministry," says Judy. "They get to see who else uses their rooms, cabinets, and space. They exchange phone numbers and build relationships."

For other appreciation event ideas, try these:

● **Volunteer Appreciation Month.** Declare a month with five Sundays as "Volunteer Appreciation Month." Do special things for volunteers on each of the five Sundays. On the first Sunday, give each volunteer a long-stemmed rose as he or she arrives at church. On the second Sunday, feature your church volunteers' pictures in a full-page appreciation ad in your local newspaper. On the third Sunday, have parents serve a "thank you" breakfast to the volunteers before church services begin. On the fourth Sunday, have children present a "thank you" service for all the volunteers in lieu of regular Sunday school classes. And on the fifth Sunday, have the senior pastor call all the volunteers to the front of the sanctuary as the congregation applauds uproariously. Then have the pastor pray for all the volunteers.

● **Show Time.** Put together a slide show or video presentation showing volunteers interacting with children. Play the song "Thank You for Being a Friend" as the images roll.

● **Balloonfest.** Give volunteers helium balloons to keep with them in the worship service. Georgia Bergstrom, a children's minister in Longwood, Florida, has her children's ministry logo and the word "volunteer" printed on their balloons.

● **Candle With Care.** Say "Thank you" with a special video featuring the music of Ray Boltz. *Thank You by Ray Boltz: A Music Video Tribute to Sunday School Teachers* is sure to leave most volunteers misty-eyed. Tie in this video with a candlelight service or a slide show of volunteers with children and you'll have even more impact. The video is available from Group Publishing, Inc., (1-800-447-1070) for $9.99. Or, Mary Van Aalsburg, a children's minister in Fresno, California, suggests having a volunteer sing this song in your church service while volunteers stand.

Birthday Ideas

Birthdays are an opportune time to let even the most stoic volunteers know that they're special. Grab this opportunity with creative ways of saying "Happy birthday."

● **First Things First.** Be the first person to call the volunteer to sing "Happy Birthday."

● **Drive-By Birthday.** Drop by the volunteer's house, ring the doorbell, and leave a balloon bouquet with a birthday card attached.

● **Card Blitz.** Pass around a birthday card to each team member or church staff member who writes a personal birthday note to the volunteer. Or have volunteers write and mail the birthday person individual cards for a birthday deluge of delight!

● **Give a Gift.** For a meaningful birthday gift, donate money to your volunteer's favorite charity in his or her name.

● **Team Birthday.** Get all your volunteers on board the birthday wagon. Distribute a list of birthdays to volunteers. Have each person create a birthday celebration for the person whose birthday comes immediately after his or her birthday. For example, a volunteer could decorate the birthday person's room, send a card, bring in cupcakes for the volunteer's class, or place flowers in the sanctuary in honor of the volunteer.

Thanking Families

Your volunteers don't carry out their ministry in isolation. Every minute that volunteers spend preparing or carrying out their ministry is time away from their families. Some volunteers will quit because they feel the tug from their family when ministry becomes a threat to family happiness. As you communicate your appreciation for families' sacrifices, you enable volunteers and families to see the tremendous impact of the volunteer's ministry, thereby increasing the family's commitment to the ministry. Try these ideas to affirm families:

● **Feed them.** On a sunny day, serve a picnic lunch to volunteers and their families after church. Meet at a park or provide fun water games so the kids can have a blast.

● **Write letters.** Send a letter to the volunteer's family, telling family members about the great ministry the volunteer has had with children. Stress that such a ministry would never have been possible without the family members' teamwork.

● **Provide a movie night.** Give a volunteer's family a coupon good for a package of microwave popcorn and a free video rental at your local video store.

● **Give a treat.** Give families coupons for frozen yogurt or ice-cream cones—one for each family member.

● **Showcase families with volunteers.** The next time you recognize volunteers in a church service, invite the families of volunteers to also stand. Affirm their role in enabling their volunteer family members to give time and love to your ministry.

● **Label families as team members.** Identify family members with their connection to your children's ministry. Give each family member a button that says, "My mom's a craft coordinator!" or "My Dad holds babies on Sunday mornings!" You can make inexpensive badges with Badge-a-Minit. Call 1-800-223-4103.

● **Plan a special family day out.** For example, if a family enjoys bowling, provide coupons for several games of bowling. Or if a family enjoys biking, arrange to meet the family with refreshing snacks and ice-cold water after a long ride. The better you know volunteers, the more effective your affirmations will be.

Say It with a Smile

"Each month we put a surprise in the teachers' basket," says Judy Cooper, director of children's ministry at Village Presbyterian Church in Shawnee Mission, Kansas. "Simple things mean a lot, such as Hershey's Hugs and Kisses with a note: 'Hugs and Kisses to you for teaching this year.' Or a pack of Extra gum with 'Thanks for going the *extra* mile.' Teachers love it!"

It's a lot of fun to find little gifts to give people that say "Thank you" in a unique way. The key to using these effectively is to make a good connection with the object and the message of thanks. And then write a note explaining the connection. I remember once I received a bag of goodies from a volunteer coordinator—a tea bag, an apple, and a balloon. It was nice, but to be honest, I didn't get it. What was the volunteer coordinator trying to say to me? She missed out on a great opportunity to affirm her volunteers with her kind gifts.

Imagine all the things a tea bag could say: "You're our children's ministry's 'cup of tea'!" or "You're totally tea-riffic!" or even "You deserve a break! Have a cup of tea and remember how you've warmed kids' hearts with Jesus' love."

What about the apple? You could say, "Here's an Apple for an Absolutely Awesome teacher!" or "An apple a day may keep the doctor away, but your teaching each Sunday keeps the doldrums away!"

And the balloon? Oh, my! Balloons remind me of joy, parties, and celebrations. You could write a note with any of these messages: "We celebrate you and your gifts to our children!" or "Your ministry makes kids want to pop with joy!" or "Every day in your class is like a big party! Thanks for celebrating Jesus with kids!"

This is fun! It's even more fun when you pull a group of people together and wildly brainstorm the options. In fact, a fun way to begin your affirmation program is to bring in dozens of items and set them on a table. Hang newsprint on the walls. Work item by item and have your creative team brainstorm about three to four ways to use each item as an affirmation. Write every suggestion on the newsprint. You'll never run out of ideas for the year!

Here are sixteen fun ideas and messages to get your pump further primed:

● Serve Good Humor popsicles at a volunteer meeting, and thank your entire team for their sense of humor and laughter.

● To each volunteer, give a resealable plastic bag filled with Goldfish crackers. Attach a note that says, "You 'fisher of children,' you're worth your weight in gold!"

● For a special volunteer, write on a box of Zesta crackers, "You add zest to our program!"

● Serve Whoppers candies at a brainstorming meeting because you know your volunteers will come up with whopper ideas.

● After a particularly tough time for a volunteer, deliver a bag of lemons or a pitcher of lemonade. Say, "Thanks for making lemonade out of a lemon of a situation!"

● On a box of Butterfinger BB's candy nuggets, write, "Thanks for sharing nuggets of truth with our kids" for each teacher.

● Give a chocolate-loving volunteer a meaningful container overflowing with Hershey's Hugs and Kisses candies. For example, if the person loves to fish, fill a fishing tackle box; for a music lover, fill a CD carrier; or for a gardener, fill a watering can. Attach a big note that says "We love you! Hugs and Kisses!" with kids' signatures.

● Deliver a Bit-O-Honey candy bar with a note that says, "You're a bit of honey to us!"

● Teachers will appreciate a 5th Avenue candy bar with this note: "Your teaching would stand out on Fifth Avenue!"

● For a sports enthusiast, write on a ball from his or her favorite sport, "Kids have had a ball in your class!"

● Serve orange juice and doughnuts to teachers before class. Post a sign that says, "Orange you glad you're teaching God's kids? We're sure glad you are! Thanks big time!"

● Give each teacher a measuring cup with this note inside. "Your teaching this year really measures up to the Master!"

● During a volunteer meeting, affirm your volunteers with tons of kudos. Tell about the great ways they've served your children's ministry. Then dump a barrel load of Kudos candy bars out in front of them—for them to keep, of course.

● On a giant bag of sunflower seeds, affirm volunteers with this note: "You've planted seeds of faith in kids' lives in a big way! Thanks!"

● On travel-size boxes of tissue, write "Your ministry to children is nothing to sneeze at. Go, girl! (or guy!)"

- For volunteer support staff, give a bag of flavored coffee beans in a special coffee cup. Attach a note that says, "Thanks! You've 'bean' so helpful! Where would we have 'bean' without you!?"

Good Job!

When a simple thank you just doesn't seem enough, use these six ideas to say thank you like you really mean it!

1. Make a banner. Work with children to create a banner for their teacher that says thank you. Have children draw pictures of their teacher doing things that they're grateful for. Then hang the banner on the front door of the teacher's home.

2. Start a chain letter. Write a thank-you note to a teacher. Attach a list of all the teacher's students and their addresses—plus the teacher's address at the bottom. Send the note and list to the first person on the list, explaining that this person must write a note and pass it on in the same way. Have the last person on the list mail all the notes to the teacher. (You may need to involve parents in this process, too!) Keep a copy of the list to monitor where the process may break down. Allow two to three days for each student.

3. Invite a few teachers to a special dinner. When the teachers arrive, they will find their students gathered for a special potluck in honor of the teachers. Include a few adults for "crowd control."

4. Food of the month. Enlist any cooks in your church to give gift certificates for the "pie," "cookie," or "bread" of the month. Tell volunteers that this is an ongoing way to say thank you to them for their service to children. Then each month on the same Saturday, have cooks gather to make the treat of choice and deliver it on Sunday morning to the volunteers.

This affirmation is a great way to say an extra big thank you to your coordinators and those volunteers who help you oversee the ministry. Doing a little more for those volunteers who do a little more affirms something my husband, Mike, continually teaches our children. That lesson is that with added responsibility come greater privileges. It's good for all your volunteers to see this as an occasional extra bonus.

5. Maitre d'. Cater a surprise breakfast for your teachers. Before teachers arrive, set up tables and decorate with nice tablecloths, china, and a long-stemmed rose in a vase. Have parents serve the breakfast—fathers in tuxedoes and mothers in black pants or skirts and white shirts. When teachers arrive, escort them into your breakfast area. Have other parents lead children in games, music, and stories.

6. Secret pals. Set up a secret pal exchange. This can either be volunteer to volunteer, or church member to volunteer. Have secret pals send their volunteers cards, notes, and gifts. Encourage them to pay attention to each other's special days and pray for each other.

Group Affirmations

Develop an atmosphere of appreciation by facilitating times for volunteers to speak good words to one another. Try these ideas:

● **Inside-outside circle.** Have volunteers form two circles—one inside the other. Have the inside circle of people face out and the outside circle of people face in. Each person should be facing another person. Tell volunteers to say one affirming thing to the person they're facing. Both people should speak. Then have people in the outside circle rotate to their right one person. Continue until people return to their starting place.

● **Circled.** This activity is best with people who know each other well. Form groups of five (or have each ministry team form a group) and have each group form a circle. Have one person at a time stand in the middle of the circle while the people in the circle tell contributions the person has made that they appreciate.

● **Affirmation wall.** Cover an entire wall in your education building with newsprint. Write your volunteers' names all over the newsprint. Leave a supply of markers. Invite parents, volunteers, children, and church staffers to write encouraging notes next to each volunteer's name.

● **Pass the praise.** Have volunteers sit in a circle. Have each volunteer write his or her name at the top of a sheet of paper. Then pass the papers around the circle and have each person write one quality they appreciate in the person whose name is on the paper. For example, people may write qualities such as "creativity, energy, ideas, passion, or dedication." Continue passing the papers until they return to their original owners.

● **Pat on the back.** Tape sheets of paper to volunteers' backs. Then

SCRIPTURE PRAYERS

Pray these verses for your volunteers. Send volunteers a card to let them know what you've prayed for them as a way to encourage them.

Ephesians 1:15-19	Philippians 1:9-11
Colossians 1:9-12	1 Thessalonians 3:12-13
2 Thessalonians 1:11-12	Philemon 4-7

have volunteers mill around and write on each paper affirming things they've seen in the person wearing the paper.

Scripture Cards

Encourage your volunteers with scriptural messages on handmade or computer-generated cards.

- **Totally Competent.** On the outside of the card, write:

"You are competent! May you find your confidence and freedom in the Holy Spirit's working in your life."

On the inside of the card, write:

"Such confidence as this is ours through Christ before God. Not that we are competent in ourselves to claim anything for ourselves, but our competence comes from God. He has made us competent as ministers of a new covenant—not of the letter but of the Spirit; for the letter kills, but the Spirit gives life."

—2 Corinthians 3:4-6

- **Wholly Complete.** On the outside of the card, write:

"You are lacking nothing—whole and complete."

On the inside of the card, write:

"But you were washed, you were sanctified, you were justified in the name of the Lord Jesus Christ and by the Spirit of our God."

—1 Corinthians 6:11

- **Concertina.** On the outside of the card, write:

"Jesus is singing joyous songs about you!"

On the inside of the card, write:

"The Lord your God is with you, he is mighty to save. He will take great delight in you, he will quiet you with his love, he will rejoice over you with singing."

—Zephaniah 3:17

- **Gift-Wrapped.** On the outside of the card, write:

"What a gift! You are a child of the king!"

On the inside of the card, write:

"He predestined us to be adopted as his sons through Jesus Christ, in accordance with his pleasure and will—to the praise of his glorious grace, which he has freely given us in the One he loves. In him we have redemption

through his blood, the forgiveness of sins, in accordance with the riches of God's grace that he lavished on us with all wisdom and understanding."
–Ephesians 1:5-8

MONEY SAVERS

The more volunteers you have, the more expensive this important ministry of appreciation becomes. But if you don't appreciate volunteers, they won't stay around for long. Here are a few ideas to help you afford year-round affirmations:

• **Budget for it.** When you're creating your budget for the coming year, add in an appreciation item with adequate funds allocated to this area. Keith Johnson, the children's pastor at Wooddale Church in Eden Prairie, Minnesota, has an annual budget of $4,000 for appreciation. Keith has 550 volunteers that minister to twelve hundred children. Keith sends notes weekly to encourage volunteers. He provides nice name tags for volunteers and spotlights volunteers in church publications.

• **Ask for financial help.** Ask people in your church who have a special interest in Christian education to donate money to purchase affirmation items.

• **Ask for donations.** Write a letter to a manufacturer asking for affirmation items to be donated. Remember, you have not because you ask not. The worst thing that could happen is that the company could say no. But many companies have overruns of products that they must take a loss on at the end of the year. It's to the company's advantage to get a tax deduction by donating these items to a non-profit organization—such as your church!

How do you find these companies? When you find items in stores that you'd like to have, but can't afford, look for the manufacturer's name and mailing address on the item. Especially look for dated or seasonal items that manufacturers may not be able to sell in the coming year. Those are the things they'll be most motivated to get rid of.

Tell the manufacturer about your church, your programs, how these items will be used, how many items you need—and offer to send them a picture of how the items are used. Be sure to provide any company that donates items with a receipt for tax purposes.

Thanks a Million

Well, maybe not quite a million, but here are oodles of quick ideas that will help you celebrate your volunteers.

1. Give a gift certificate from a local restaurant.
2. Have children use a permanent marker to sign a thank-you T-shirt.
3. Give two movie tickets.
4. Give a small plant.
5. Personalize a tote bag.
6. Clean a teacher's classroom.
7. Fill a coffee mug with a bag of ground flavored coffee.
8. Create a bulletin board that features volunteers serving children.
9. Have Psalm 71:18 printed in calligraphy and framed for a volunteer: "Even when I am old and gray, do not forsake me, O God, till I declare your power to the next generation, your might to all who are to come."
10. Give Whoppers candies with this note: "Thanks for your whopper ideas!"
11. Give a relaxing bath experience with a gift of bubble bath or scented, floating candles.
12. Give a prayer journal with a personalized note written in the inside jacket.
13. Give a cookie cutter with a note that says, "Thank you for molding kids' lives."
14. Give a seed packet with a note that says, "Wow! You're planting God's Word in young children's hearts!"
15. Give plastic visors with "Top Volunteer" painted on them.
16. Give a Mounds candy bar with this note: "You're making a mound of difference!"
17. Call a different team member each day just to see how the person is doing.
18. Ask for reports on past prayer requests.
19. Go to lunch with a volunteer—a different person each week.
20. Invite a volunteer over for dinner.
21. Send an encouraging note with a Scripture verse.
22. Share a valuable children's ministry resource.
23. Offer to help a volunteer move—better yet, plan a moving party for a team member.
24. Take your volunteers on a retreat.

25. Send a thank-you card with a personalized note.
26. Plan a team fun day where the church picks up the tab.
27. Establish convenient parking places for "volunteers only."
28. Create a comfortable coffee area for volunteers only. Provide fresh pastries and fruit.
29. Give a Bar None candy bar with this note: "Bar none, you're the best!"
30. Greet each volunteer by name.
31. Smile.
32. Personalize greetings with statements such as "Hey, friend!"
33. Mention a person's contribution in your church bulletin or newsletter.
34. Provide child care for volunteer training times.
35. Use chalk to write volunteer affirmations on the sidewalk leading to your church so everyone can celebrate the good things your volunteers do.
36. For a volunteer who coordinates a big event or program, send a bouquet of roses to that volunteer at church.
37. Write a personalized letter from Jesus to the volunteer. For ideas, see the "Personalized Letter From Jesus" box (p. 117).
38. Believe in people. Say, "I know you can do it!"
39. Rent a horse-drawn carriage to parade your volunteers around your church.
40. Give a volunteer his or her favorite dessert.
41. Give Life Savers candies with this note: "You're a real lifesaver."
42. Frame a favorite photo for a volunteer.
43. Clip and send a funny cartoon or joke that a volunteer will appreciate.
44. Give a journal for a volunteer to keep track of the paths of God in their ministry.
45. Hug a volunteer.
46. Give your volunteers children's ministry "business" cards.
47. Plaster a thank-you note on a marquee.
48. Give a book of stamps with this note: "You're a special delivery from God!"
49. Give a container of wild berries that you picked yourself. Attach this note: "You're berry special!"
50. Give a certificate for eighteen holes of golf to a golfer with this note: "You're a hole-in-one for our children's ministry!"
51. Give a new fishing lure to someone who loves fishing with this note: "Our children's ministry is hooked on you!"
52. Volunteer to baby-sit while a couple goes out for a date.

53. Wash a volunteer's car—and clean the inside too.

54. Offer to do one task for a volunteer that'll reduce her stress, such as running errands.

55. Give a bag of peanuts with this note: "We're nuts about you! Thanks for bringing kids out of their shell."

56. Mow a volunteer's yard—or in the fall you can rake leaves.

57. Hold a thank-you card shower for a special volunteer.

58. "Kidnap" a volunteer for breakfast.

59. Take kids over to weed a volunteer's garden.

60. Give the gift of a back massage from a professional massage therapist.

61. Give a coupon for a latte and scone at a trendy coffee shop.

62. Enlist a prayer supporter for each volunteer who'll contact them regularly to discover prayer needs.

63. Give a sports enthusiast two free tickets to his or her favorite professional team's game.

64. Share your "frequent flyer" miles with a volunteer.

65. Give a Baby Ruth candy bar with this note: "You're a real slugger! Keep on batting for children."

66. On Saturday morning, deliver the best cinnamon rolls in town for a volunteer's entire family.

67. Point out one specific thing that you appreciate about a volunteer's approach to ministry.

68. Compliment a volunteer in front of parents.

69. Introduce the volunteer with an honoring statement, such as "Sue is a gifted and creative preschool teacher," not simply "Sue is a preschool teacher."

70. Fax a thank-you letter to a volunteer in the middle of the week, pointing out something wonderful you saw in them on Sunday.

71. Use paint pens to personalize jars for your volunteers. Then encourage people to regularly drop in encouraging notes for the volunteers.

72. At a volunteer meeting, have volunteers write their names on cards. Then have them trade cards and write a completion to this statement: "Without you, our ministry would…"

73. Call a volunteer's answering machine to leave a message about how much you appreciate him or her.

74. Pray for your volunteers every day.

75. Sign up to take a meal when a volunteer has had a life situation that creates a need.

76. Have children make "hand-print" aprons or sweatshirts for volunteers.

77. Have kids make Christmas cards for their teachers. A painted hand print on the cover is the perfect decoration.

78. Give animal crackers with this note: "This place would be a zoo without you."

79. Give pretzels with this note: "We'd be in knots without you."

80. Give a 100 Grand candy bar with this note: "You're worth even more than this to us!"

81. If you see a volunteer's name in print, cut it out and send it with a note that says, "Brown" hits the headlines again! Your ministry should be in lights!"

82. Send a Scripture verse with a thank you note that says how you've seen the person living out the verse in ministry.

83. Make a handmade certificate affirming the person's contribution.

84. Make an acrostic of the volunteer's name with the things you've seen in them that you've appreciated. For a volunteer named Tom, your acrostic might read:

T-eaching gifts

O-bedience to God in answering his call to ministry

M-ega fruit in the lives of children.

Seasonal Affirmations

Follow this plan to go the extra mile during every season of the year.

● **New Year's.** Give volunteers a devotional book to encourage their

faith throughout the year. Enclose a bookmark in it. I made this bookmark for the volunteers at our church in three easy steps:

1. Using Microsoft Publisher, I created a design page with eight bookmarks.

2. I placed a clip-art apple at the top of each bookmark. Then I centered this quote under the apple and down the bookmark:

"A teacher affects eternity; he can never tell where his influence stops."

—Henry Adams.

3. I printed the bookmarks on red paper and had them cut apart and laminated.

● **Valentine's Day.** Create Valentine's Day cards for your volunteers. Glue a red construction paper cross to the front of your card. Then glue a white heart to the cross. On the inside of your card, print this poem:

No roses or candy, I send to your door.

Nor trinkets or violets, My love means much more.

I send a golden sunrise, And my constant watchful care, Eternal, fresh, unchanging, So my love you may share.

Love eternally,

Jesus.

● **Easter.** Make cinnamon flower hangers for volunteers. Mix together 1 cup applesauce, 1½ cups cinnamon (check natural food stores for cinnamon sold in bulk), and ⅓ cup nontoxic glue. Form a ball and refrigerate overnight. Sprinkle a little cinnamon on a cutting board, roll out the dough to ¼-inch thick, and use flower-shaped cookie cutters to cut out flowers. Use a plastic straw to punch out a hole at the top of each flower. Allow flowers to dry for two days. Then tie a red ribbon hanger through the hole in each flower.

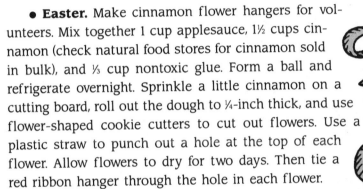

Write each volunteer a note on floral stationery telling how you've seen God's love blooming in children's hearts.

● **Back to School.** Help your volunteers be even more creative with a year's subscription to Children's Ministry Magazine. Call 1-800-447-1070 to subscribe for $24.95.

● **Thanksgiving.** Give the gift of food—spiced nuts to be precise. With this idea, you can also attach a note that says, "We're nuts about you and your ministry to children!"

For each volunteer, you'll need ½ pound of pecans, ⅙ cup unsalted butter, ⅙ cup sugar, ¼ teaspoon each of cinnamon and ground sugar, ⅛ teaspoon each of ground nutmeg and ground cardamom, ⅛ teaspoon ground cloves, and a pinch of salt.

Toast the pecans in a preheated 300 degree oven for 15 minutes. Combine the butter and sugar in a saucepan. Cook over low heat, stirring until the butter melts. Then stir in the other spices.

Pour the butter and spice mixture over the pecans and toss until the nuts are well coated. Bake for 30 minutes at 300 degrees. Cool completely.

Place the nuts in quart-sized resealable plastic bags to deliver to volunteers.

● **Christmas.** Make lamb ornaments for your volunteers to thank them for their service to God's little lambs. For the volunteers in our church, we're making these lambs from Family Fun magazine. To make one, you'll need white or black yarn, a 3x4-inch piece of stiff cardboard, a rubber band, scissors, a square of black felt, glue, a small gold belt, a black chenille wire, red ribbon, and an embroidery needle.

To make the body, loosely wrap the yarn around the width of the rectangle until it's covered at least three times. The more yarn, the fluffier the sheep. Then slide the yarn onto your fingers, gathering all the loops together. Put a rubber band around the loops, cinching it like an hourglass. Cut through the loops on both ends and fluff up the pompom. Shear the sheep if the ends are uneven.

Cut a face shape—with a long face and ears—out of the felt. Glue the face and bell onto one end of the sheep. Cut the chenille wire in half and thread the two pieces through the center of the sheep's body to create legs.

For a hanger, cut a ten-inch length of ribbon, fold it in two, and knot the two ends together. Thread the unknotted end of the loop through an embroidery needle and pull it up through the center of the sheep. The knot will catch on the sheep's body to create the hanger.

So cheer, affirm, honor, praise, commend. and applaud your volunteers. Use these ideas to celebrate the dedicated people who make your ministry possible. May God bless you as you seek to bless others in your ministry to children.

Stop & Consider

Want to affirm your volunteers, but can't find the right words? Why not let God do the talking? Check out what Scripture has to say about God's children (your volunteers!).

As children of God, we are
favored (Psalm 5:12),
protected (Isaiah 25:4),
beautiful (Isaiah 61:10),
loved (Jeremiah 31:3),
salt (Matthew 5:13),
valued (Matthew 6:26),
light (John 8:12),
secure (Romans 8:31),
triumphant (Romans 8:37),
gifted (Romans 12:6),
cleansed (1 Corinthians 6:11),
competent (2 Corinthians 3:5),
new creations (2 Corinthians 5:17),
alive (Galatians 2:20),
forgiven (Ephesians 1:7),
God's workmanship (Ephesians 2:10),
chosen (Colossians 3:12), and
enabled (1 Thessalonians 5:24).

Send notes with these words from God to volunteers. Or plan an entire event to celebrate the good things that God says about your volunteers. You could post these on signs around your room, write them on place mats, or give one calligraphied verse to each person.

Way to Go! Good Job!

SHOWING APPRECIATION

Affirmations are a distinctive part of Bonnie Newell's ministry at Breiel Boulevard Church of God in Middletown, Ohio. Bonnie describes her appreciation ministry to the 150 volunteers she manages.

"Volunteers need to feel appreciated on an ongoing basis. They're the core of the ministry of the church and their faithfulness needs to be recognized on a regular basis. We often find in churches that we spend a great deal of energy getting and keeping the visitor or new person and neglect the long-time person who has volunteered many hours in service to the Lord.

"Specific things I've done:

"I use a 'TeacherGram' postcard regularly to jot a short note to my volunteers that I do appreciate them. Sometimes I send these in the mail or leave them in the teacher's mailbox. On special occasions, I send a message with a piece of candy attached.

"I use a 'CareGram' in the same way for volunteers who aren't teachers, such as assistants, secretaries, or superintendents.

"I send a card that says, 'Today, I prayed for you' to let the teachers know that they're in my prayers. I have all these cards printed ahead of time. I simply fill it out and drop it in the mail after I've prayed for someone. I want my teachers to feel the strength and encouragement of knowing that someone is praying specifically for them.

"I give a bouquet of balloons to my classroom teachers. I use disposable helium tanks and balloons. I tie an appreciation note to each small bouquet of balloons, and then I place the bouquets in classrooms before teachers arrive.

"I give a gift to each teacher at Christmas. I try to find inexpensive gifts such as a Christmas mug with candy in it or Christmas pins. Many times I find the gifts for the next year at after-Christmas sales the previous year. I attach a personal appreciation note with the gift.

"I give flowers to the children's choir director on opening night of any program. This is a great way to affirm all their time and leadership with our children.

"The key to success in the ministry of affirmation is consistency. The most sought-after commodity in today's society is time. I want my volunteers to know that I appreciate them placing ministry in the church at the top of their list as they prioritize their time. I want volunteers to feel that God has placed them in this area of ministry and I appreciate all that they do."

PERSONALIZED LETTER FROM JESUS

I received the following letter from a special friend named Anne Herrington while I was in seminary. I've adapted it for you.

Dear Loved One:

Who are you? You are the loved one of the Supreme Ruler of all—loved with limitless, perfect love that never fluctuates or changes.

What are you like? In me, you are valuable and desired—included forever.

Where are you going? What is the meaning of your existence? I have given you the greatest destiny possible—to be my very own for all time and eternity—sharing my love and purposes. You are somebody because somebody loves you!

I love you, my friend! Believe that today—I shed my own blood for you. You stand forgiven before the Almighty King. You are precious in my sight. Whenever you get discouraged or down on yourself, remember that my grace is sufficient and my mercies are never ceasing. Remember that I promise to meet your needs according to my riches and fulfill your desires with good things.

Look to me. It's in me that you'll find fullness of joy and pleasures forever. You are so loved! You are a special creation—unique and wonderfully designed by God's perfect hands. I have a plan for you. I will use you.

Remember that I am slow to anger and abundant in loving kindness. You are my chosen child and you share in my treasures. All I have is yours too! I have filled you with my love, my joy, my peace—walk in my victory today!

Relax in my grace—cease striving. Let me do all through you.

Jesus

Conclusion

I hope this book has helped you as you seek to shepherd the volunteers in your children's ministry. It's never easy, but the rewards are eternal. And even though at times we may feel like we labor alone, Scripture promises that the Holy Spirit will be with us to help and guide us in the ways of the Master, Jesus. John 14:26 says: "But the Counselor, the Holy Spirit, whom the Father will send in my name, will teach you all things and will remind you of everything I have said to you."

So even when you feel discouraged, don't give up! Galatians 6:9 says: "Let us not become weary in doing good, for at the proper time we will reap a harvest if we do not give up." Keep recruiting, keep training, keep investing in your volunteers. In his time, God will provide a harvest—in the hearts of your workers, and in the hearts of the children they serve.

APPENDIX 1

SAMPLE JOB DESCRIPTION
CHILDREN'S SUNDAY EDUCATION TEACHER

Qualifications
1. Grow in Christian character and relationship with Jesus Christ.
2. Attitude of service not only toward children, but also toward their parents and other staff workers.
3. Knowledge and understanding of the developmental needs and characteristics of children.
4. Supports the statement of faith in the church constitution.

Functions
1. Be present in the department at least fifteen minutes before class time begins.
2. Prepare a well-developed lesson plan weekly.
3. Participate in all scheduled teacher training and planning meetings.
4. Secure a substitute teacher when needed, reporting your absence and replacement to your Department Team Leader and/or Age-Level Coordinator.
5. Maintain contact with your learners.
6. Suggest recruitment prospects to the Department Leader.
7. Provide an environment that will foster spiritual growth among your team workers and learners.
8. Evaluate the progress of each student throughout the year.

Accountability
Report directly to your divisional coordinator. A review will be conducted semiannually.

Term of Service
This position will be appointed for a term of nine months.

Volunteer's signature: _____ Date: _____
Ministry overseer's signature: _____ Date: _____

(Adapted by permission from Larry Schweitzer at Evangelical Free Church of Naperville, Naperville, Illinois.)

APPENDIX 2

Sample Volunteer Application Form

Name: _____

Address: _____

City/State/ZIP: _____

Telephone: _____

Fax: _____

E-mail address: _____

Driver's license number: _____

Social Security number: _____

Occupation: _____

Employer: _____

Your birth date: _____

Marital status: _____

Spouse's name, if applicable: _____

Children's names and ages, if applicable:

_____

_____

Desired position: _____

Program: _____

Position: _____

Age level: _____

Last ministry experience (program/position/age level):

_____

_____

Church membership status (circle one):
Member   Visitor   Regular Attender

How long have you been attending/or a member of our church?

_____

List the names and addresses of churches you attended regularly over the last seven years:

Write a brief statement of your Christian faith:

Please provide two nonfamily personal character references (these people must be from outside our church):

Name: _____   Name: _____
Address:_____   Address: _____
City: _____   City: _____
State/ZIP: _____   State/ZIP: _____
Telephone:_____   Telephone: _____

Have you ever been arrested for, convicted of, or pleaded guilty to a criminal act? _____ If so, please explain:
_____
_____
_____

I affirm to the best of my knowledge that the information on this application is correct. I authorize any reference or church listed on this application to supply any information that may pertain to my character and fitness to work with children. I hereby release any organization or individual from any liability from any damages that I may incur.

Signature: _____ Date: _____

(Adapted by permission from Debbie Neufeld Grant Memorial Baptist Church, Winnipeg, Manitoba.)

APPENDIX 3

Reference Check Form

Name of Applicant: _____

Address: _____

City/State/ZIP: _____

1. How long have you known the applicant and in what capacity?

2. How well do you know the applicant?
___very well ____well ____casually

3. Comment on any area of the applicant's family background that would help our understanding of the applicant.

4. Comment on the applicant's personality and character.

5. From your experience, how well suited is the applicant for working with children?

6. From your experience, where is the applicant on his/her spiritual journey?

7. Would you recommend this applicant with
____enthusiasm _____reservations _____not at all

Name of Reference: _____

Church: _____

Address: _____

City/State/ZIP: _____

Interviewer's Signature: _____ Date: _____

(Adapted by permission from Debbie Neufeld Grant Memorial Baptist Church, Winnipeg, Manitoba.)

APPENDIX 4

Motivating Through Gifts

Gift	Definition	Motivational Comments
Administration	To organize, plan, and execute procedures to meet ministry goals.	"Wow! We could never have pulled off our VBS without your organizational skills! Your ability to foresee problems made everything go smoothly!"
Serving	To express God's practical love for people's day-to-day needs.	"Thanks for setting up and decorating for our Fall Festival. The kids were delighted with all the fun things you created. It made our event very special!"
Teaching	To understand God's Word clearly and apply it to listener's lives.	"The kids in your class are so well-grounded in the Word of God. I'm confident that they have a good foundation in truth!"
Exhortation	To encourage and move people to action in their faith.	"I want you to know that Jane's mom said she has grown so much in her faith as a result of your class. Your ministry to her has changed the way she acts at home!"
Giving	To contribute money and resources to promote God's work.	"Christmas would not have been possible without you pointing out the needs in this one family. Thank you for spearheading a generous ministry to them!"
Shepherding	To help groups of people grow and minister to others.	"It is such a delight for your team to follow your leadership. God has certainly gifted you in this area!"
Mercy	To meet the needs of those in distress or crisis.	"Thank you so much for ministering to Ann when she was crying. I'm so grateful for your gift to be able to speak to people's hearts."

APPENDIX 5

Team Leader Report

Monthly Report for Team Leaders

Month of:

MINISTRY AREA	PLAN	EVALUATION
Prayer—What things are you consistently praying for your team members?		
Training—What skills or character development do your team members need? What's your plan to meet those training objectives?		
Encouragement—What will you do this month to affirm, celebrate, or encourage your team members?		
Relationship—What activities will you do with your team members to build friendships? When will you do these?		
Accountability—What areas of growth do you need to check back on with team members from the previous month?		

APPENDIX 6

Individual Training Chart

Name:

Present Situation	Goal	Forces Helping	Forces Hindering	Steps to Goal

Group Publishing, Inc.
Attention: Product Development
P.O. Box 481
Loveland, CO 80539
Fax: (970) 669-1994

Evaluation for *Awesome Volunteers*

Please help Group Publishing, Inc., continue to provide innovative and useful resources for ministry. Please take a moment to fill out this evaluation and mail or fax it to us. Thanks!

● ● ●

1. As a whole, this book has been (circle one)

not very helpful   very helpful

1   2   3   4   5   6   7   8   9   10

2. The best things about this book:

3. Ways this book could be improved:

4. Things I will change because of this book:

5. Other books I'd like to see Group publish in the future:

6. Would you be interested in field-testing future Group products and giving us your feedback? If so, please fill in the information below:

Name _____

Street Address _____

City _____ State _____ Zip _____

Phone Number _____ Date _____

BRING THE BIBLE TO LIFE FOR YOUR 1ST- THROUGH 6TH-GRADERS...
WITH GROUP'S HANDS-ON BIBLE CURRICULUM™
Energize your kids with Active Learning!

Group's **Hands-On Bible Curriculum**™ will help you teach the Bible in a radical new way. It's based on Active Learning—the same teaching method Jesus used.

In each lesson, students will participate in exciting and memorable learning experiences using fascinating gadgets and gizmos you've not seen with any other curriculum. Your elementary students will discover biblical truths and <u>remember</u> what they learn because they're <u>doing</u> instead of just listening.

You'll save time and money, too!

While students are learning more, you'll be working less—simply follow the quick and easy instructions in the **Teacher Guide**. You'll get tons of material for an energy-packed 35- to 60-minute lesson. And, if you have extra time, there's an arsenal of Bonus Ideas and Time Stuffers to keep kids occupied—and learning! Plus, you'll SAVE BIG over other curriculum programs that require you to buy expensive separate student books—all student handouts in Group's **Hands-On Bible Curriculum** are photocopiable!

In addition to the easy-to-use **Teacher Guide**, you'll get all the essential teaching materials you need in a ready-to-use **Learning Lab**®. No more running from store to store hunting for lesson materials—all the active-learning tools you need to teach 13 exciting Bible lessons to any size class are provided for you in the **Learning Lab**.

Challenging topics each quarter keep your kids coming back!

Group's **Hands-On Bible Curriculum** covers topics that matter to your kids and teaches them the Bible with integrity. Switching topics every month keeps your 1st- through 6th-graders enthused and coming back for more. The full two-year program will help your kids...

- •make God-pleasing decisions,
- •recognize their God-given potential, and
- •seek to grow as Christians.

Take the boredom out of Sunday school, children's church, and midweek meetings for your elementary students. Make your job easier and more rewarding with no-fail lessons that are ready in a flash. Order Group's **Hands-On Bible Curriculum** for your 1st- through 6th-graders today.

Hands-On Bible Curriculum is also available for
Toddlers & 2s, Preschool, and Pre-K and K!

Order today from your local Christian bookstore, or write: Group Publishing, P.O. Box 485, Loveland, CO 80539.

Exciting Resources for Your Children's Ministry

No-Miss Lessons for Preteen Kids
Getting the attention of 5th- and 6th-graders can be tough. Meet the challenge with these 22 faith-building, active-learning lessons that deal with self-esteem...relationships...making choices...and other topics. Perfect for Sunday school, meeting groups, lock-ins, and retreats!

ISBN 0-7644-2015-1

The Children's Worker's Encyclopedia of Bible-Teaching Ideas
New ideas—and lots of them!—for captivating children with stories from the Bible. You get over 340 attention-grabbing, active-learning devotions...art and craft projects...creative prayers...service projects... field trips...music suggestions...quiet reflection activities...skits...and more—winning ideas from each and every book of the Bible! Simple, step-by-step directions and handy indexes make it easy to slide an idea into any meeting—on short notice—with little or no preparation!

Old Testament   ISBN 1-55945-622-1
New Testament   ISBN 1-55945-625-6

"Show Me!" Devotions for Leaders to Teach Kids
Susan L. Lingo

Here are all the eye-catching science tricks, stunts, and illusions that kids love learning so they can flabbergast adults...but now there's an even *better* reason to know them! Each amazing trick is an illustration for an "Oh, Wow!" devotion that drives home a memorable Bible truth. Your children will learn how to share these devotions with others, too!

ISBN 0-7644-2022-4

Fun & Easy Games
With these 89 games, your children will *cooperate* instead of compete—so everyone finishes a winner! That means no more hurt feelings...no more children feeling like losers...no more hovering over the finish line to be sure there's no cheating. You get new games to play in gyms...classrooms...outside on the lawn...and as you travel!

ISBN 0-7644-2042-9